TAXIDERMY
STEP BY STEP

TAXIDERMY
STEP BY STEP

by Waddy F. McFall

with drawings and photographs by the author

WINCHESTER PRESS

Photographs on p. 210 are reproduced courtesy of
the American Museum of Natural History

Library of Congress Catalog Card Number: 75-9263
ISBN: 0-87691-209-9

Library of Congress Cataloging in Publication Data
McFall, Waddy F
Taxidermy step by step.
Includes index.
1. Taxidermy.   I. Title.
QL63.M23   579'.4   75-9263
ISBN 0-87691-209-9

Published by Winchester Press
205 East 42nd St., New York 10017
Printed in the United States of America

Contents

Acknowledgments

No book on taxidermy would be complete without giving credit to those most responsible for developing it to its present level. It would be quite impossible to list all of those who have contributed in some way, but the undisputed leader in the field has to be the late Carl E. Akeley, who did more to develop and improve taxidermic methods than anyone before or since his time.

Most of Mr. Akeley's life was devoted to the development and improvement of taxidermy, particularly large mammal work. Many of the methods he invented and perfected have since been simplified to some extent, but not necessarily improved. He was the originator of the sculptured-model and hollow-manikin method of taxidermy. Before his time, taxidermy consisted mostly of crudely stuffing skins with straw, excelsior, or anything else that was handy, and the finished product bore little resemblance to the living animal. One of Mr. Akeley's greatest contributions was also his ability to inspire and develop the talents of the people who worked with him.

Carl Akeley died in Africa in 1926 while on one of many expeditions to collect specimens for the African Hall in the American Museum of Natural History. This hall now stands as a memorial to him.

I never had a chance to know Mr. Akeley personally, since he was a little before my time. A few years later, however, I was fortunate enough to know and work with several of the men who had been close friends and protégés of his, and who were carrying on the work that he had started at the American Museum of Natural History. All of these men—Dr. James L. Clark, Robert H. Rockwell, Raymond B. Potter, Louis P. Jonas, and others— seemed to have inherited much of Mr. Akeley's boundless energy and almost uncanny ability. I am deeply grateful to these men and to all others who have done their share to promote and improve taxidermy.

—W. F. M.

Introduction

If you are a beginner in taxidermy, you are about to launch into a fascinating pastime that will give you many hours of pleasure as a hobby, or perhaps later as a profession. Taxidermy as a hobby is usually more satisfying than commercial taxidermy. The commercial taxidermist must make a profit to stay in business, and must sometimes concentrate on production at the expense of quality. The hobbyist, on the other hand, can strive for perfection without the pressure and responsibilities that influence the commercial taxidermist.

As you gain experience and confidence, the work will become easier and more pleasurable. The important thing in the beginning is not to become discouraged if your first few efforts are not entirely satisfactory. The methods and procedures are not difficult to learn, but there is absolutely no substitute for practice and experience.

It is good to visit other taxidermists whenever possible. After more than forty years' experience in both museum and commercial taxidermy, I still find it very beneficial to visit other taxidermists, and seldom do so without learning something of interest or value.

No one knows all there is to know about taxidermy. There are few, if any, hard-and-fast rules to follow. The animal world offers so many types and varieties of mammals, birds, reptiles, and fish that no single method of taxidermy will be entirely satisfactory for all of any one category. Most of the problems to be encountered are fully discussed in the text; but as you work on more and more types of specimens, other problems are likely to present themselves from time to time. However, by applying the knowledge you will gain here, plus a little ingenuity and common sense, the problems can be overcome.

Although this book was written primarily for beginners, more experienced taxidermists will also find parts of it useful and profitable.

I have tried to cover each phase of taxidermy as clearly and simply as possible, giving step-by-step directions. In cases where more than one method is commonly used to accomplish the same job I have described each method. You may pick the one that seems easiest to you or that best suits your needs. All of the methods described here can give excellent results or poor results. The success of any method depends largely upon the skill of the operator.

Do not accept any method as final. If you can think of a better way, do not hesitate to try it. In almost every field of work, new methods and techniques are being discovered and tried every day. A new and better method often seems so obvious that one has to wonder why it was not thought of years before. As time goes by I hope you will develop new ideas and methods of your own, for this is how progress is made.

TAXIDERMY
STEP BY STEP

Collecting and Care of Specimens in the Field

The importance of proper care of specimens to be mounted cannot be overemphasized. In commercial work we usually have no control over the care and handling of specimens before they reach our studio, but how nice it would be if we did.

Literally thousands of beautiful specimens are practically ruined each year before they reach a taxidermist. This happens through both ignorance and carelessness. Even though poorly handled specimens can usually be mounted, the quality of the finished product is sometimes not what it should be, and the amount of time and effort required to do the job is greatly increased. Even slight imperfections in a specimen before it is mounted often become much more noticeable after it is mounted. Following are some brief tips on collecting and caring for specimens immediately after they have been collected.

BIRDS

Unfortunately, most birds to be mounted must be collected by shooting. This is not always bad, but some will be unavoidably mutilated.

When hunting birds for mounting, especially small birds, it is best to use a shotgun of small gauge, loaded with the smallest shot available. A .410, 20-gauge or 16-gauge gun, loaded with No. 10 shot, is usually satisfactory. Try to shoot the bird at the greatest distance at which you can be fairly sure of bringing it down.

After the bird is down, examine it carefully. The mouth, vent, and any bleeding shot holes should be plugged immediately with cotton, paper, or scraps of cloth to prevent blood or body fluids from soiling the feathers. Fresh bloodstains can usually be easily removed with a damp cloth.

Note carefully the color of the eyes, beak, feet, and any other fleshy parts. These areas sometimes fade or change color in a short time, and the correct colors must be restored after mounting.

Always allow the body heat to dissipate as quickly as possible. The bird should be carried by the feet so as not to ruffle the feathers any more than necessary. After it has cooled, it is good to roll the bird in a sheet of newspaper, if available. This keeps the feathers clean and prevents them from being damaged.

Birds should not be skinned until they are thoroughly cool. If the body heat is still present it is much more difficult to keep fluids from getting on the feathers while skinning.

If the weather is warm, and the bird is not to be skinned for several days, it should be refrigerated. If it is necessary to keep the bird for some time, it should be put in a plastic bag or wrapped in aluminum foil and frozen. Birds should never be drawn before skinning; this only soils the plumage and makes the job of skinning more difficult.

Birds which are obtained alive may be killed in several ways without damaging the skin. One method is to use either chloroform or ether. To use this method, a sheet of paper is rolled into a cone shape. Place a wad of cotton or cloth down in the small end of the cone and saturate it with chloroform or ether. Place the bird's head down in the cone and hold it securely for a few minutes until the bird is dead.

In most states the sale of chloroform and ether is prohibited except to members of the medical profession. If you are permitted to buy these chemicals in your locality, always use them with extreme caution.

Another simple method of killing a bird is to grasp the body just below and behind the wings. Press firmly with your thumb on one side and your middle finger on the other. This will cut off the bird's air supply and kill it in a few minutes.

Remember that most birds in the United States are protected by either state or federal laws, or both, and may be legally taken only by special permit, or in some cases, not at all.

SMALL MAMMALS

Small mammals may be taken either by shooting or trapping. The smaller species, especially, are usually in better condition for mounting when they have been trapped rather than shot; but sometimes, of course, this is not possible.

Common steel traps are not usually good for taking specimens to be mounted because they often damage or mutilate a leg almost beyond repair unless you use the traps designed to kill the animal quickly. There are, however, some types of traps that are much more humane, and do not damage the skin.

The common spring-and-board-type mouse and rat traps are inexpensive, and are quite effective in taking small animals up to the size of a weasel. There are also several live animal traps on the market which are effective, but rather expensive.

You can make your own live animal traps which work about as well as any, and cost almost nothing, if you have some scrap lumber. See Fig. 1.

These traps are very effective in catching rabbits, opossums, and other animals of similar size. Larger versions can also be made for catching larger animals. It is better to make traps out of old lumber rather than new, and it also helps to camouflage them by partially covering them with leaves and small branches. Bait which will be attractive to the animal you are trying to catch should be placed in the back of the trap so the animal will have to brush by the trigger in order to reach it. In some cases it is better to tie the bait to the trigger.

The cleanest, and generally the safest, way to kill an animal caught in a box trap is by drowning. A rabbit can be easily killed by holding it up by the hind legs with one hand and giving it a sharp blow across the back of the neck with the edge of your other hand.

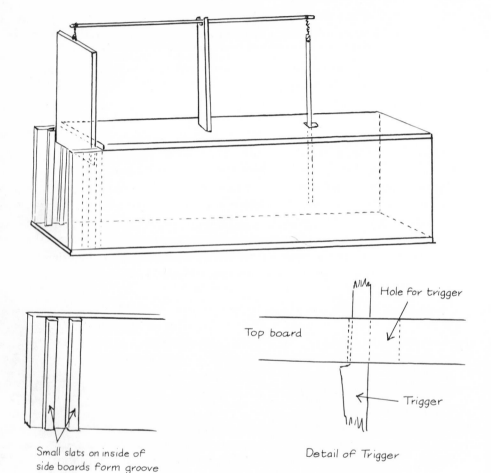

Small slats on inside of side boards form groove for door.

Detail of Trigger

FIG. 1   A box trap that can be used for catching small mammals without damaging the skin.

It is not advisable to try this on any animal except a rabbit, however.

When approaching a sprung box trap, proceed cautiously until you can tell what is inside. If you happen to have a skunk it most likely will not have discharged its scent unless a dog or some other animal frightened it after it was caught. Do not make any loud noises or do anything to scare the animal. Pick the trap up carefully and carry it to the nearest water that is deep enough to cover the whole trap. Gently, but quickly, push the trap under the water and hold it there until the animal has had plenty of time to drown.

This is about the only way to kill a trapped skunk without danger of its discharging its scent, and it is an equally effective method of killing other animals.

Fig. 18 in Chapter 3 shows the location and anatomy of the scent mechanism of a skunk. It would be well to study this before skinning such an animal.

As strange as it may sound, about the most effective remover of skunk scent is tomato juice. If you have a skin with some scent on it, you can wash the skin in tomato juice, then in plain water, and this will usually kill the odor.

Ordinarily, small mammals do not require as much care in the field as birds, since fur can be more easily washed and cleaned than feathers. It is always best, however, to keep any specimen as clean as possible. In warm weather, when there is danger of spoilage, a small mammal may be gutted or skinned in the field. This is not usually necessary, however, unless you plan to be out for more than a few hours.

Small mammals, like birds, should be allowed to cool as quickly as possible. Body heat will cause a skin to spoil more quickly than artificial heat. Once the hair starts to slip on an animal, there is little chance of saving it.

Instructions for skinning small mammals are given in Chapter 3.

LARGER MAMMALS

Under this classification, I include animals the size of a bobcat or larger. These can, of course, be skinned in the field or brought in whole, depending upon the temperature and circumstances. Ordinarily, if the animal is to be mounted whole, it is better to bring it in whole so you will have the carcass in your shop to study and take measurements from while you are making the artificial body. If this is not possible or practical, you should make enough sketches and measurements in the field to enable you to reproduce a fairly accurate model. If you cannot save the whole carcass, perhaps you can save the leg bones and skull, which will be a great help.

When out on a hunting or collecting trip, a pencil, notebook, and measuring tape should be standard equipment, as well as your gun and skinning knife. If you are to be out for several days, you should also carry some salt along in case it is necessary to salt down hides in camp. This is true except in damp tropical climates where skins are usually best dried in a cool, shady place without the use of salt. In any case, skins should be completely skinned and fleshed before being salted or dried.

Complete instructions for skinning game heads and large mammals are given in Chapter 4.

FISH

When collecting fish for mounting it is important to make color notes as soon as possible after the fish is taken from the water. A handy method for doing this is shown in Fig. 78 in Chapter 12. Color slides are also helpful when restoring the colors to mounted fish.

Unless absolutely necessary, do not gut a fish in the field. If the specimen can be kept cool and damp, it will keep just as well without gutting. If the fish must be gutted, however, always cut it on one side instead of down the middle in the belly.

Fish should always be kept damp and out of the sunshine. Loose-scaled varieties should not even be handled with dry hands, and the fins on any variety should never be allowed to dry until the specimen is mounted.

If no ice is available, freshly caught fish may be wrapped in wet paper, cloth, or even moss, and then in several layers of dry newspaper. This is good insulation, and will usually keep a fish damp and in good condition for several hours, even in hot weather.

If well wrapped to prevent dehydration and fin breakage, a fish may be kept frozen almost indefinitely without damage.

REPTILES AND AMPHIBIANS

The collecting or handling of reptiles holds little appeal for many people, while to others it is fascinating. Mounted reptiles always attract attention; therefore, they can be good advertising. It is usually worthwhile to have a few mounted ones on display.

It is a good idea to become familiar with the species of reptiles found in the locality in which you are hunting, and to know which ones can be handled safely. Until you can recognize the poisonous species, of which there are but few, you should exercise extreme caution in collecting snakes.

Reptiles and amphibians should be captured alive whenever possible, as they tend to deteriorate rapidly after death. When collecting such specimens you should carry along some heavy cloth bags to keep them in.

The easiest and best way to kill these specimens without damaging them is to have them in cloth bags and place the bag in a freezer overnight. This is painless, and does not damage the specimen in any way. They can be quickly thawed in cool water when you are ready to work on them.

Most frogs and many snakes, especially the water snakes, can be most effectively hunted at night.

The easiest way to capture many frogs is to wade a small stream or shallow pond at night, and scan the edge of the water and bank with a spotlight. A frog's eyes can often be seen glowing as they reflect the light. When you spot a frog, approach him from the front, very quietly, and keep the light focused on him at all times. When you get close enough, grab him around the middle with one hand, and hold tight.

Sometimes, many water snakes are seen on a night frog-hunting trip, but they are usually much harder to catch than frogs. There are several species of water snakes found in the United States. They are all harmless, except the cottonmouth moccasin, which is native only to the southeastern states from Virginia southward through Florida, and around the Gulf Coast to eastern Texas. They also range up the Mississippi Valley as far as southern Illinois. They are sometimes difficult to distinguish from the harmless varieties, so one should be very careful about latching onto any water snake in cottonmouth areas unless you are absolutely sure what you are getting. The harmless varieties do not have fangs or venom. They do have many small holding teeth, however, and are harmless only as far as venom is concerned. Most of them are rather ill-tempered, and will bite viciously even though their bite is not dangerous.

If you are going to collect snakes, it would be wise to take along some extra equipment. Fig. 2 shows two tools which are widely used by snake hunters. They are both designed to hold and keep a snake at a safe distance until you can safely catch it behind the head with your hand. That is the only safe place to hold a snake that wants to bite; even then, accidents can and often do happen. No novice is advised to capture or handle poisonous snakes.

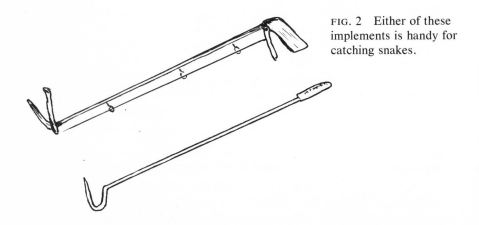

FIG. 2   Either of these implements is handy for catching snakes.

2

Skinning and Mounting Birds

To one who has not tried it, the skinning of a bird might seem an impossible task. Actually, most birds are easier to skin than most mammals. It is true, however, that some species are much more difficult than others, and for this reason, it would be best for the beginner to start on one of the easier kinds.

A common pigeon is an excellent specimen to practice on. They are a convenient size, have a fairly tough skin, and are easily obtained in most localities. If you are unable to get a pigeon, a magpie, crow, quail, or even a well-feathered chicken will do. A pheasant is also an excellent bird to work on; in fact, they are about the easiest of all birds to skin.

Before starting to skin a bird, a fresh plug of cotton should be placed in the mouth, vent, and any other openings from which body fluids may escape. Have the necessary tools ready, and also a small container of borax or cornmeal.

Lay the bird on your workbench with its head to your left. Separate the feathers along the breastbone. On most birds there is a bare area down the center of the breast where no feathers grow.

With your knife or scalpel, make an incision from the forward end of the breastbone to the vent, as shown in Fig. 3. Be careful to cut only through the skin, not deep enough to go into the body cavity.

Lift one edge of the cut skin and separate it from the body. Cut any membranes that may be holding the skin to the body, and separate the skin from the body as far as possible on each side. Sprinkle borax or cornmeal on the exposed body as you proceed. If the bird is to be used for food, use cornmeal; otherwise, you may use borax. The purpose of using either of these is to absorb any moisture on the body, thereby helping to keep the feathers dry and clean.

Hold the skin away from the body on one side of the incision and push the leg on that side up so that the joint between the thigh and drumstick is exposed. Cut through this joint, leaving the thigh attached to the body, and the remainder of the leg in the skin.

Using your scissors or bone snips, cut through the base of the tail just below the vent, being careful not to cut through the skin on the back. You may now peel the skin from the entire rear end of the body.

At this point, it is much easier if you hang the bird up. This may be done with a hook and chain set or merely by tying a string around the body in front of the thighs and hanging it from above. See Fig. 4.

After the bird is hung, proceed with the skinning until you reach the wings. Cut through the joint connecting the wing to the body on each side, and pull the skin on down over the neck and head.

On some birds it is possible to pull the skin right on over the head to the base of the beak. On other birds—those which have large heads or topknots—this is not possible. On these birds the head must be skinned through an incision on the top of the head, as will be explained later.

Pull the skin gently as you reach the forward end of the neck. If the base of the skull is easily exposed and it appears that you can pull the skin on over the head, proceed cautiously. Carefully cut the membranes around the ear openings and keep pulling until the eyes are reached. Carefully cut the membrane that connects the eyelids to the skull, being careful not to cut the eyelids. Pull the skin on down to the base of the beak.

The head may now be cut off where the neck joins the skull. Remove the eyeballs, being careful not to puncture them. The fluid

FIG. 3 Breast incision for skinning bird. This and the other steps in mounting a bird are also illustrated in the sequence of photographs that appears later in this chapter.

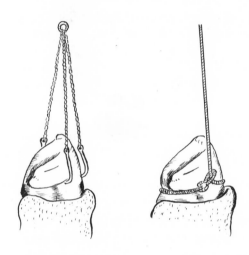

FIG. 4 Two methods of hanging a bird for skinning after the rear end of the body has been exposed.

in the eyes is hard to remove if it gets on the feathers. Cut and scrape all flesh from the skull, but leave the bone intact. Slightly enlarge the opening to the brain cavity, where the neck was cut off, and remove the brain. This can be done with a brain spoon, but a small piece of wire bent into the shape of a hairpin generally works better. Small bits of cotton twisted in the end of a wire can also be used to swab out the brain cavity.

When you have the skull cleaned, coat it generously with powdered borax. Do not overlook the brain cavity. Now you are ready to turn the skin right side out. If the neck and head skin has dried out somewhat, moisten it with borax water until it is soft and pliable again. Now, push the skull back through the neck skin. This can easily be done by placing the tips of your thumbs against the back of the skull and working it carefully back through the skin.

If your bird is one with a large head that could not be skinned as described above, make an incision as shown in Fig. 5. Skin the head through this incision, and clean the skull as already described.

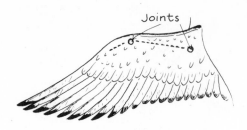

FIG. 5   Head incision for birds with large heads or topknots.

FIG. 6   Dotted line shows incision on underside of wing.

The incision on the back of the head may be left open until the bird is mounted.

You are now ready to finish skinning the legs and wings. The ends of the upper wingbones are plainly exposed inside the skin. Hold the end of this bone and pull the skin back until the whole bone is exposed down to the first joint. Cut all flesh from the bone, but do not remove the bone. Repeat the operation on the other wing. The flesh from the remaining two joints of the wing must be removed by making incisions on the underside of the wing as shown in Fig. 6. These incisions must be sewed up if the bird is to be mounted with spread wings; otherwise, it is not necessary to sew them.

The legs must now be skinned. The ends of the drumstick bones are exposed inside the skin. Hold the end of this bone and pull the skin down to the first joint. If the feathers grow below this joint, you can skin on down almost as far as the feathers grow. Remove all flesh from the leg bones, but do not sever the joints.

Next, make a small incision on the bottom of each foot. Insert an awl, a nail, or any such instrument under the tendons in the bottom of the foot, and pull the tendons out of the lower leg. See Fig. 7.

Your skinning job is now almost complete. Examine the inside of the skin carefully and remove any remaining flesh that may be attached to the skin. Trim the flesh from the base of the tailfeathers, but be careful not to dislodge the feathers. If the skin is very fat in places, scrape these areas with a knife or spoon, and remove as

FIG. 7   To remove tendons from the lower leg, make a small incision and pull them out with a pointed tool, tweezers, pliers, or some other instrument.

much of the fat as possible. Sometimes it helps to put a little gasoline or acetone on the fatty areas as you scrape. This will dissolve much of the fat and make it easier to remove. If too much oil or fat is left in the skin it will eventually work through and soil the plumage.

In scraping bird skins, always scrape from rear to front. By doing this the roots of the feathers are not as likely to be damaged.

Some birds, particularly ducks and geese, often have much fat incorporated in the skin itself. No amount of surface scraping will remove this. On such skins you can take a sharp knife and carefully score the skin, in a checkerboard pattern, between the roots of the feathers. Be very careful not to cut the skin all the way through; cut just enough to score the fatty tissue. After you do this you can scrape lightly, adding a little gasoline or acetone from time to time to help dissolve the fat. Cornmeal or borax also helps to soak up the excess oils. After you have removed as much fat as you can, the skin should be given a thorough cleaning with gasoline and plaster as described below.

CLEANING BIRD SKINS

Fresh bloodstains can usually be removed from the feathers with a damp cloth or a piece of cotton. If the stains have dried, they are much more difficult to remove. Badly stained areas can usually be cleaned by washing them with warm water to which a little detergent has been added. The liquid detergent commonly used for washing dishes works quite well. Do not wash the whole skin in this; just dip the badly soiled feathers and gently rub them between your fingers until the stain is loosened, then rinse them in plain water. After rinsing, the feathers can be dried by squeezing them between paper towels or blotters. The feathers can then be further dried and fluffed by working them in powdered borax.

Bird skins which are not fat, and which have been kept clean during skinning, may be mounted without further cleaning. However, if the skin contains an appreciable amount of fat, or if the feathers appear dirty or matted, the entire skin should be thoroughly cleaned.

To do this, place the skin in a vat and completely saturate it with gasoline. Be sure that all parts of the skin are wet with the gasoline.

Pick the skin up by the beak, and with your other hand, carefully squeeze out the excess gasoline, working from the head toward the tail.

When the excess gasoline has been removed, place the skin in a box and add any kind of dry plaster of Paris. Use plenty of plaster and work it thoroughly into the feathers and skin. The plaster quickly absorbs the remaining gasoline in the skin. Add more plaster if needed, until the feathers appear quite dry.

Take the skin out of the plaster; shake it vigorously, and beat it with a small, slender stick until all the plaster has been removed. If you have an air compressor or a vacuum cleaner with a blower attachment, use this. The remaining plaster can be blown out of the feathers much more quickly and thoroughly than by shaking and beating.

The first time you try this cleaning process it will seem that you have ruined the skin for sure until the process is completed. The results are highly satisfactory, however; and skins treated in this manner come out clean, fluffy, and in excellent condition for mounting.

You can keep a box of plaster on hand to use just for cleaning bird skins. The gasoline will soon evaporate out of the plaster, and it will not be necessary to use fresh plaster each time. Do not try to use this plaster for any other purpose, however.

CAUTION: Always remember that gasoline is explosive and

should not be used carelessly. Also, the above cleaning process is quite dusty, and should always be done out of doors.

When you have finished cleaning the skin, moisten the inside with borax water, and apply borax liberally to the inside.

If your first attempt at skinning and preparing a bird skin is successful, you should be congratulated. If it does not turn out as well as you hoped, do not be discouraged. Each successive attempt will become easier, and you will soon be able to prepare a skin in a fraction of the time it took to do the first one.

Once you have a good skin it can be mounted immediately or put away for future mounting. If it is necessary to keep the skin for more than a day or two, it should be put in a plastic bag and frozen rather than allowed to dry out. If the skin is allowed to dry, however, it can be relaxed by wrapping the feet in wet cloth or paper, and filling the skin with damp paper or cloth for several hours or longer. A bone-dry skin is sometimes quite difficult to relax and prepare for mounting. It is much better to mount the skin while it is fresh, if possible.

MOUNTING BIRDS

Unlike most phases of taxidermy, the method of mounting birds has changed but little through the years.

Taxidermy supply houses are now selling bird bodies made of paper, plastic, and other materials. They advertise them as being great timesavers, but with a little practice you can make an excelsior body in the time it takes to send off an order. Furthermore, the excelsior body costs almost nothing and works as well as or better than the commercially made bodies.

Your excelsior should be of fine grade for small birds, and fine or medium grade for larger birds. It should be dampened by sprinkling or dipping in water before you start. This will make it pack better and thereby make a much firmer body.

Use either the natural body or outline drawings and measurements of the natural body as a guide.

Take a handful of the damp excelsior and twist it firmly to form a hard core. Fold the ends back so the core is about the same length as the natural body, not including the neck. Wind this core with string to hold it tightly together. Keep adding damp excelsior and winding with string until the artificial body is built up to the dimensions of the natural body. Do not try to put too much detail modeling into the excelsior body; just concentrate on getting it smooth and to the same general outside dimensions as the natural body. See Fig. 8.

You are now ready to insert the neck wire. Select a piece of galvanized wire of the proper size for the specimen you are working on. (See table at the end of this chapter.)

The neck wire should be 5 or 6 inches longer than the natural body and neck, and should be sharpened on both ends. Insert one end of this wire into the neck location on the artificial body, and force it all the way through until it comes out the rear end. Bend a hook in the tail end of the wire and push the sharpened end of the hook back into the artificial body, thereby anchoring it firmly.

The neck is built up by winding cotton or tow around the neck wire out to the proper length. This wrapping should be put on in rather thin layers, and each layer wound with string until the neck is built up to the proper size.

Notice the curve of the natural neck, and bend the neck wire into the same general curve. Refer to Fig. 8 again. The final bending of the neck wire will be done after the bird is mounted, but it is usually helpful to bend it slightly beforehand.

If you have not already decided on the position in which the bird is to be mounted, you should do so now. One of the most common faults to be seen in mounted birds is that the legs are often placed in the wrong position on the body, This gives the bird an unnatural appearance, and spoils what otherwise might be an excellent mount.

This mistake can easily be avoided if you understand how a bird moves its legs when it walks, and if you mark the proper position of the leg wires on the artificial body before you insert it in the skin. Study the natural body, and notice how the thighbone moves in an arc. Imagine how the position of this bone would be as the bird assumes different positions. Remember that the leg wire must be attached to the body somewhere along the arc formed by the forward end of the thighbone. Fig. 9 shows how the position of the leg wires will vary according to the position of the bird.

When you have decided where the leg wires should be placed, put an ink mark on each side of the artifical body to show the exact

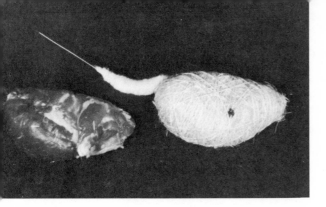

FIG. 8 A natural body and an excelsior body. The inked spot on the excelsior body is where the leg wire is to be inserted.

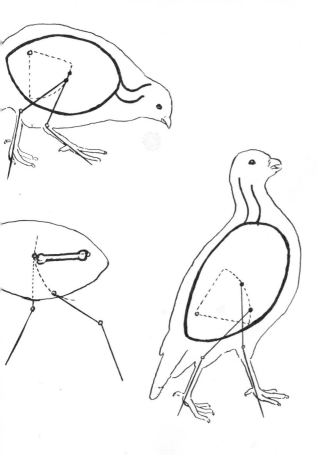

FIG. 9 The forward end of the thighbone moves in an arc as a bird assumes different positions. This should be taken into consideration when inserting the leg wires.

spot where the wire should be inserted. Also, put an ink mark where the wing wires are to be placed. This point does not vary as in the case of the legs, but when the artificial body is inserted in the skin it is sometimes very difficult to judge exactly where the wire should go unless the spot is marked.

When you have the artificial body completed, and the correct position of the leg and wing wires established, you are then ready to proceed with the mounting.

Examine the skin. If it has dried in places, apply a little borax water. Expose the skull again and place a small ball of cotton or tow in each eye cavity. Also, place a thin layer of cotton over the skull, letting it extend down over the sides of the skull, and tuck the ends of the fibers between the lower jawbones. Many people do not do this, but it is a good practice. The cotton acts as a cushion between the skin and the skull, and keeps the bird from having a shrivel-headed appearance after the skin dries.

Next, you will need wires for the legs and wings, if the wings are to be wired. If the bird is to be mounted with spread wings, the wings must, of course, be wired. If the wings are to be closed, it is not absolutely necessary to wire them, but it is definitely a better practice to do so except on very small birds.

In cutting the leg wires, allow enough wire to extend the length of the leg, plus enough more to be anchored through the body, plus still enough more to attach the bird to the base it is to be mounted on. The leg wires need to be sharpened on only one end.

Insert the sharpened end of the wire into the ball of the foot, and push it up through the leg just back of the leg bone. Since you have previously removed the tendons, the wire will go easily to the first joint. Work it past the joint and on up alongside the drumstick bone.

Tie the drumstick bone and wire loosely together with string. With cotton or tow, proceed to wrap the bone and wire to replace the muscles of the leg. This wrapping should be fairly firm, but not so tight that the leg wire cannot be slid easily. Put a few turns of string around the wrapping to hold it in place, and then pull the skin back up over it. Repeat this with the other leg.

The wing wires must be long enough to extend the length of the wing, plus enough more to anchor through the body. These wires must be sharpened on both ends.

Insert the wing wires from inside the skin. Run the wires alongside the bones the entire length of the bony structure, and on out the tip.

Tie the wire loosely to the upper wingbone, and replace the muscles on this bone with cotton or tow just as you did on the legs.

When both wings are wired in this manner you are ready to insert the artificial body.

Run the neck wire up through the neck skin until it reaches the skull. Feel through the skin with your fingers, and guide the wire into the opening of the brain cavity. If the bird's head was skinned through an incision on top of the head, you can do this by sight rather than feel. Hold the head at an angle so that the wire will pierce the top of the skull; then push the wire through the top of the skull and out through the skin on top of the head until the neck wrapping is seated in the back of the skull.

Pull the skin down over the neck until the artificial body lies in the proper place in the skin.

Force the wing wires through the artificial body at the ink marks you made previously. Angle the wires so they go through enough thickness of the body to give strength. Bend a hook in the ends of the wires, and pull the sharpened ends of the hooks back into the body to anchor them firmly.

When the wires are anchored, hold the outer end of the wire and push each wing toward the body so that the end of the large wingbone is seated firmly against the body.

FIG. 10   Bird skin with legs and wings wired, ready for the artificial body. The dark spots on the body show where the leg and wing wires are to be inserted.

Next, insert the leg wires through the body and anchor them in the same manner. Push the ends of the leg bones firmly against the body, and bend the legs down so the feet point toward the tail.

The breast incision can now be sewed up. Start sewing at the tail end, and insert the needle from the inside of each stitch so as not to pull the feathers through the skin with the thread. If the artifical body has been made correctly, the skin should fit snugly, but without tightness. If the skin seems to be too loose, you can place a layer of cotton over the breast before sewing up the incision.

When the incision has been sewed up, you can start to shape the specimen to the desired position. If the wings are to be closed, bend them at the joints and fold them against the body.

The bird should now be placed on either a temporary or a permanent perch. Drill holes in the perch to receive the leg wires. Be sure that the holes are the right distance apart, so the bird will stand in a natural position. Run the leg wires through these holes and bend them underneath or fasten them in some way to make the bird stand steady on the perch. You can then proceed to shape the bird into the proper position.

Bend the legs as needed to make the bird stand properly. The wings may also need some additional adjusting. The feathers can be smoothed and arranged by lifting them with a sharp wire or a pair of tweezers.

To make the tail stay in the proper position, bend a sharpened wire into the shape of a T, and insert the sharp end into the body just under the tail. This wire may be hidden under the feathers and left permanently, or it may be pulled out later when the skin is completely dry.

If the bird is to have spread wings, arrange them in the desired position, then sew up the incisions that were made on the underside. It will usually be necessary to support the wing feathers in some way until the skin has dried. If necessary, you can stick a sharpened wire into the side of the body, and curve the wire under the long wing feathers to keep them from sagging. The other end of the wire may be twisted around the end of the wire which is still protruding from the tip of the wing. You should also pin strips of cardboard on the upper and lower surfaces of the wing to hold the feathers securely in place while the skin is drying. If the tail is to be spread, do it in the same manner. See Fig. 11.

FIG. 11   If the bird is mounted with wings and tail feathers spread, pin cardboard strips as shown to hold the feathers in position while the skin dries.

After a bird with closed wings is shaped to your satisfaction, it should usually be wrapped with string to hold the body feathers in place until the skin dries. See Fig. 12. Small sharpened wires or pins can be stuck into the bird wherever necessary to keep the string from slipping off.

If the bird has been mounted on a permanent perch, the toes should be pinned in a natural position until they are dry and stiff. If you have used a temporary perch, the toes should not be allowed to dry out until the bird has been changed to a permanent base. In

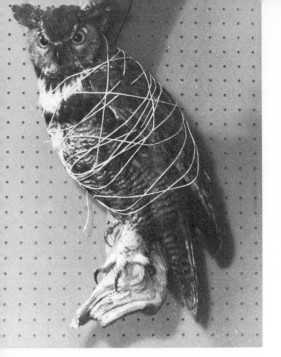

FIG. 12 If the bird is mounted with closed wings, tie them with string to hold the feathers in place. Sometimes cardboard strips are needed for the tail, as in Fig. 11.

case the toes do become dry, and you wish to change their position later to fit another perch, they can be wrapped in wet cloth or cotton for a day or two until they are flexible again.

If the head was skinned through a head incision, it should be sewed up during the shaping process. You can add a little cotton around the base of the skull if needed. This incision should be sewed carefully by inserting the needle from the skin side; do not pull the stitches so tight as to make the feathers stand up along the seam.

FINISHING THE SPECIMEN

After the bird is completely dry, which will ordinarily take about two weeks, it is ready for the finishing touches.

Carefully remove the string wrapping or cardboard strips, and pull out any pins or wires that might have been used to hold the string in place. With a pair of side cutters, carefully cut off the wires that protrude from the head and wings.

Refer to your color notes and touch up the feet, beak, eyelids, and any other fleshy parts that may need it. The type of paint or stain to use for this is best determined by the nature and texture of the area to be colored and the amount of actual color that is actually needed to give the right effect. Unless a lot of pigment is needed to replace the colors that have faded or darkened in drying, it is generally best to thin your paint down so that it acts more as a stain than a paint. Most taxidermists probably use oil colors for touch-up work. These colors can be thinned with turpentine as needed and are generally satisfactory. Sometimes, however, other types of colors work better and dry much faster.

Acrylic paints can be used with good results. These colors come in tubes like oil colors and are used in the same way except that they are thinned with water instead of turpentine, and they dry in a few minutes instead of a few days.

In some instances, lacquer or various dyes can be applied with an airbrush to give a most natural appearance. Another paint that works quite well is Testor's Pla Enamel, which comes in small bottles and can be bought in most hobby shops.

A TYPICAL BIRD, START TO FINISH

The series of photographs that follows shows a hawk from the first incision to the finished mount. There are special problems with some birds; these are discussed later in this chapter. However, you do not have to try one of the more difficult birds for your first attempt. The only difficulties with the hawk are that the head is large and must be skinned through a top incision, and that the eye structure is unusual.

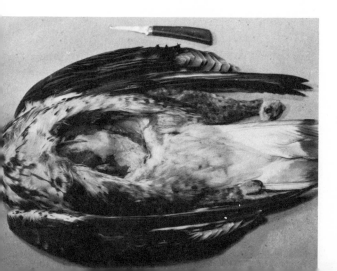

1 Make the breast incision and pull the skin back on each side to expose the body.

2 Disjoint the legs between thigh and drumstick. The base of the tail may also be severed at this stage.

3 The entire rear end of the body is now exposed and suspended from above. At this point the wings may be disjointed from the body.

4 After the wings are disjointed, pull the skin down over the neck to the base of the skull. On many birds the skin can be pulled on down to the base of the beak by carefully cutting the membranes around the ear openings and the eyes. Since this hawk is a large-headed bird, the neck should be cut off at the base of the skull and skinned later through a head incision.

5 Skin the legs out and remove the flesh from the drumstick bones. Then skin the upper wingbones in the same manner.

6 Skin the remaining wingbones by making incisions on the undersurface of the wings and stripping the flesh from the bones.

7 Remove the tendons from the lower leg by making an incision in the bottom of the foot and forcefully pulling them out.

8 The head in this case is skinned by making an incision on the back of the head skin. The picture shows one eye removed. (See Fig. 14, later in this chapter, for a diagram of the hawk's eye structure.) The brain is removed through the opening where the neck joined the skull. As much flesh as possible should be scraped from the skull. The skinning is complete when you have removed any remaining fat and flesh from the skin. Before proceeding with the mounting, the skin should be thoroughly cleaned with gasoline and plaster if it is very oily or badly soiled. Otherwise, all inside parts must be liberally treated with borax or arsenic before mounting.

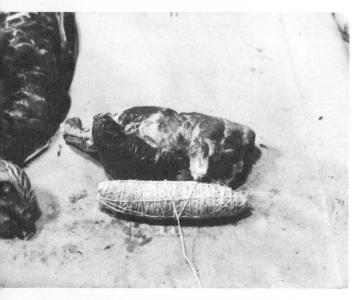

9 Make an artificial body by twisting a core of damp excelsior the approximate length of the natural body and wrapping it tightly with string. Keep adding excelsior and winding with string until the body is built up the same size and general shape as the natural body.

10 This shows the artificial body with the neck wire inserted and ready to be anchored.

11 After you have wired the legs and wings and wrapped the bones with tow and string to replace the flesh that was removed, the skin is ready to receive the artificial body. Notice that the points where the leg and wing wires are to be inserted have been marked on the artificial body.

12 Put the artificial body inside the skin and anchor the leg and wing wires in place. The breast incision can now be sewn up.

13 After the breast incision is closed, place the bird on either a temporary or a permanent perch and bend the legs, wings, and neck into the desired position. The head incision should also be sewn at this time.

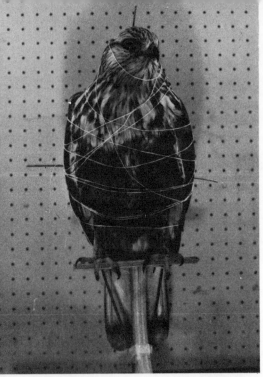

14 When the bird is shaped
to your satisfaction it
should be wrapped lightly
with string to help hold
the feathers in place until
the skin dries. The end of
the neck wire, which is
protruding through the
top of the head, may be
cut off now or later. The
wires sticking from the
sides of the body were
inserted during the
wrapping process to help
hold the wings in place
and to keep the string
from slipping. These
wires are pulled out later.
Artificial eyes of the
proper size and color may
be set in place now.

15 The finished mount.
When the specimen is
completely dry, restore
the color to any fleshy
parts with paint or stain.

MISCELLANEOUS INFORMATION

Balsa-Wood Bodies: When mounting small birds, especially, it is often better and easier to make the body of balsa wood instead of excelsior. It is sometimes difficult to wind a very small body of excelsior and make it firm enough to hold the wires securely. Balsa wood is light, firm, and easy to carve, and there will be no danger of wires becoming loose. It is good for making bodies for larger birds also, but the excelsior is probably easier and faster to use for larger specimens.

Back-Incision Skinning: In skinning birds which have white breast feathers, or very sparsely feathered breasts, it is sometimes desirable to use the back-incision method. Some taxidermists use this method almost exclusively, but there is no real advantage in it except in the above-mentioned cases.

In this method the skinning is done as previously described except that the incision is made down the back instead of the breast.

Birds with Combs or Wattles: Birds such as chickens, turkeys, and others which have combs, wattles, or both have always presented somewhat of a problem for taxidermists. These parts, which cannot be skinned, are often just allowed to dry and shrink as they will, but this results in a sorry-looking job at best.

The proper way to handle these parts is to make a mold of them while they are still fresh and full. A cast is made from the mold in either wax or plastic and attached to the bird.

Instructions for making molds and casts are given in Chapter 9. The quickest and best way to make a mold of soft, fleshy parts, however, is to use the dental impression material described in Chapter 11. This material gives fine detail and is ready to use in minutes. The cast to be made from this impression or mold can be made of acrylic plastic, or it can be made of wax. See Formula #3.

Owls: In skinning owls you will notice a marked difference in the eye structure from that of other birds. The eye is not only larger, the eye itself is contained in a bone-rimmed container

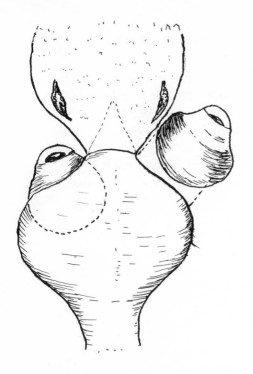

FIG. 13   Top view of an owl's skull with the skin peeled back, showing the eye structure, which differs from other birds.

which fits into the eye socket of the skull and gives a very distinct shape to the head. See Fig. 13.

In preparing the head, remove the eyes as in other birds, but do not throw them away. After the whole eye is removed from the skull, cut around the iris and empty the fluid from the eyeball or sac. Clean out this cup with a piece of cotton, and apply borax to all parts. Fill the eyecup with cotton or tow, and replace it in the eyesocket of the skull. Be sure to replace it in exactly the same position; otherwise, the face will not have the correct expression.

Hawks: Members of the hawk family also have a peculiarity about the eye that should be mentioned. Just above the eye there is a thin bone which projects out over the eye somewhat like a tiny visor. This is a part of the skull rather than the eye, but it is sometimes accidently cut off when skinning the head. Without this small bone, the face will not have the correct shape or expression. See Fig. 14. This small bone is what gives the eyes of hawks and eagles the characteristic deep-set look.

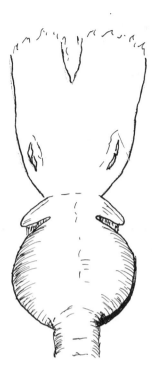

FIG. 14 Top view of a hawk's skull. Notice the little visorlike bones over the eyes. These bones should be left intact when skinning the head.

Open-Mouth Bird Mounts: Sometimes you may want to mount birds with the mouth open. In this case you should prop the mouth open when you set the mounted bird aside to dry. Notice the shape and color of the tongue of the bird when you remove it in skinning, and carve a tongue of balsa wood or some other soft wood. When the bird is dry, you can put a little papier mâché or water putty down in the throat and set the artificial tongue in place.

Long-Legged Birds: Birds with very long legs such as large herons and cranes sometimes present a problem if they are to be mounted standing on one leg. A single galvanized wire that is small enough to go through the leg is sometimes not stiff enough to give the bird adequate support. In such cases you can use a ¼-inch iron rod through the standing leg instead of a wire. One end of the rod should be sharpened and anchored in the body.the same as a wire, but the other end should be threaded and attached to the base with nuts and washers.

Damaged Eyelids: If an eyelid on the bird is damaged or accidentally cut in skinning so that it gives an unnatural appearance to the eye of the mounted bird, it sometimes helps to glue a piece of string around the glass eye. The string can then be painted like the eyelid.

Bent or Twisted Feathers: Feathers which are bent or twisted and look unsightly can often be fixed by holding them over the steam vent of a boiling kettle for a few seconds.

Recommended Wire Sizes for Various Birds

Wire Size

No. 20	English sparrow, canary, etc.
No. 18	starling, robin
No. 16	mourning dove, kingfisher, magpie
No. 15	pigeon, snipe
No. 14	small hawks, teal, screech owl
No. 13	pheasant, grouse, crow
No. 12	large hawks, large ducks
No. 10	Canada goose, great horned owl
No. 8	buzzard, eagle
No. 6	pelican

Eye Size and Color for Various Birds

	Eye size (mm.)	*Color*
American bittern	10–11	yellow
Least bittern	7–8	yellow
Blackbird (Redwing)	5–6	brown
Bluebird	4–5	brown
Blue jay	7	black
Bobwhite quail	8	hazel
Buzzard	12	brown
Canary	3	brown
Cardinal	6	brown
Catbird	6	brown
Chapparel	10	special
Chicken (domestic)	10–11	hazel
Coot	9	red
Cormorant	12	green

	Eye size (mm.)	*Color*
Crow	10	black
Dove	7	brown
Ducks		
American Goldeneye	10	yellow
Black	10	brown
Bufflehead	10	brown
Baldpate	10	yellow
Gadwall	11	brown
Harlequin	10	brown
Mallard	11	brown
American Merganser	11	red
Hooded Merganser	9	yellow
Old-squaw	10	brown
Pintail	9	brown
Redhead	10	yellow
Scoter	10	yellow
Shoveler	10	yellow
Spoonbill	10	yellow
Ruddy	11	hazel
Scaup	11	yellow
Teal, bluewing	9	brown
Teal, cinnamon	9	yellow
Teal, greenwing	9	hazel
Widgeon	10	brown or yellow
Wood duck, male	10–11	red
Wood duck, female	10	yellow
Eagle, bald, immature	16	brown
Eagle, bald, adult	17	yellow
Eagle, golden	17	brown
Flicker	7–8	brown
Grebe	8–9	red
Grouse, ruffed	10	hazel
Gulls		
Bonaparte's	9	brown
Franklin	10	brown
Herring	12	yellow
Laughing	10	red
Ringbill	10	yellow
Hawks		
Sparrow	9	brown
Cooper's	12	yellow
Marsh	12	yellow

	Eye size (mm.)	Color
Osprey	14	yellow
Goshawk	14	red
Redtail	14	yellow
Roughleg	14	hazel
Red-shouldered	14	hazel
Sharp-shinned	10	yellow
Killdeer	7	black
Kingfisher	10	brown
Loon	14	red
Magpie	8	brown
Owls		
Arctic	19	yellow
Barred	18–20	black
Barn	14	brown
Burrowing	10	yellow
Great horned	20	yellow
Long-eared	14	yellow
Pigmy	12	yellow
Screech	14	yellow
Saw-whet	12	yellow
Snowy	20	yellow
Short-eared	14	yellow
Pelican	17	yellow
Pheasant, male	11	special
Pheasant, female	10–11	brown
Pigeon	8	orange
Swan	14	brown
Turkey	13	brown
Woodcock	10	brown
Wren	2	brown

3

Skinning and Mounting Small Mammals

The method described in this chapter is generally used on medium- or long-haired animals up to the size of a skunk or opossum. Although these animals can be mounted by the methods described for larger animals, the process given here is simpler and quicker, and will produce excellent results if carefully done. Any very short-haired or sparsely haired animal which shows a great deal of muscle structure is best mounted on a sculptured form.

SKINNING

Animals to be mounted by this method may be skinned either by the ventral (belly) incision or by the dorsal (back) incision. The ventral incision is more commonly used and is perhaps a little easier. However, if the animal has very thin hair on the belly or if it is to be mounted in a position where the underparts will be in plain view, the dorsal incision should be used.

A short-haired mammal that is to be viewed from only one side, such as in a museum group, can be skinned so that no stitches will be visible from the show side. This is done by carefully planning the position beforehand and making all cuts in the skin on the blind side. This can get a little complicated at times, however; so until you have quite a bit of experience, it would be better to stay with the more conventional methods.

The ventral incision is made from the forward end of the breast-bone to the base of the tail. See Fig. 15. Peel the skin back on each side of the incision, and separate the hind legs from the body at the pelvic joints. Disjoint the front legs at their union with the should-erblades, leaving the shoulderblades attached to the body. See Fig. 16. Separate the skin from the back, toward the rear end of the body, and expose the base of the tail. The tail can usually be pulled out of the skin fairly easy by putting the base of the tail through a sturdy pair of tweezers or between the handles of a pair of scissors. Grasp the tool with one hand and the base of the tail with the other and pull. See Fig. 17.

Some animals have rather fleshy tails that cannot be pulled out of the skin in this manner. In this case, the tail must be split part of the way, or in some cases all the way, to the tip.

When the rear end of the body is free, proceed with the front end and skin on over the head. Cut the ears off close to the skull, and be careful around the eyes not to cut the eyelids. When the mouth is reached, cut in close to the teeth and remove the skin completely from the head.

The legs should now be skinned by pulling them out of the skin all the way to the base of the toes. A small incision should be made on the bottom of each foot. This will make it easier to pull the skin over the feet.

Do not disjoint the bones of the legs or feet, but strip and scrape all the flesh from them.

Examine the inside of the skin and remove all flesh and fat. Clean all flesh from the base of the ears, and cut the excess flesh from the inside of the lips. If the animal has large ears, they should be turned inside out by separating the cartilage from the skin on the back side of the ear.

When skinning members of the skunk family, be very careful not to cut into the scent glands or to put too much pressure on the glands while skinning. Fig. 18 shows the location of the scent glands and their anatomy. The mink and weasel also have scent

FIG. 15   The ventral incision on a small mammal should extend from the forward end of the breastbone to the head.

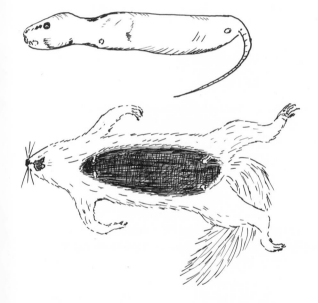

FIG. 16   Body and skin of a small mammal. Note the ends of the leg bones inside the skin.

FIG. 17   An easy method for pulling the tailbone from the skin. Grasp tweezers with left hand and pull firmly on body with right hand.

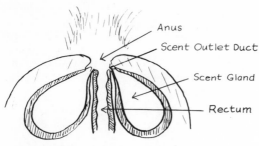

Anus

Scent Outlet Duct

Scent Gland

Rectum

Internal View from Underneath

FIG. 18   Internal and external views of a skunk's scent mechanism.

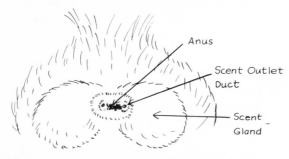

Anus

Scent Outlet Duct

Scent Gland

Rear View — Scent Nipples Extruded

glands similar to those of a skunk, but they are not as large or as highly developed and their scent does not carry as far as that of a skunk. However, in close quarters the odor is even more disagreeable.

DEGREASING

If the skin is very fat it should be degreased. This can be done in several ways. After scraping off as much fat as possible with a knife, the skin may be washed in lukewarm water with soap or detergent and then rinsed in plain water. After rinsing, squeeze out as much water as possible.

Skins that are extremely greasy should be washed thoroughly in white gasoline, and then in water as described above.

PICKLING THE SKIN

Although it is best to tan all mammal skins before mounting, it is seldom done on the smaller specimens. They must, however, be pickled in a preserving solution before being mounted.

One of the best and quickest pickles for small mammal skins is denatured alcohol. This penetrates the skin quickly, and when the skin has been in the alcohol from a few hours to a day or two it is ready to be mounted. Skins may be left in the alcohol for weeks or months without damage. Always keep the alcohol in a container with a tight-fitting lid as it evaporates quite fast. See Formula #7 in the Appendix for other pickling solutions that may be used instead of alcohol.

After the skin is taken from any pickle bath, it should be rinsed in plain water and worked in a quantity of dry borax before mounting. The borax will help to repel insects and will also help to dry and fluff the fur.

MAKING THE ARTIFICIAL BODY

Before disposing of the natural body you should use it for a model in making the artificial body or at least make outline drawings and measurements of it for later use.

The artificial body can be made of excelsior and string as described the preceding chapter for mounting birds, or, if you prefer, it can be carved of balsa wood.

First decide on the position in which the animal is to be mounted and place the carcass in that position.

Moisten your excelsior so it will pack firmly. Twist a quantity of the excelsior tightly to form a firm core the length of the natural body without the head and tail. Wrap this core with string as tightly as possible, and keep adding excelsior and winding with string until the body is built up to the size of the natural body. If the animal has rather short hair it is good to put a thin layer of cotton over the excelsior and wind it with lightweight sewing thread. This will give the body a little smoother surface. See Fig. 19.

Sharpen a wire for the tail and run it through the artificial body.

FIG. 19 An artificial body for an ermine, with excelsior body and balsa head, and the finished mount.

Bend a hook in the forward end of the wire and anchor it firmly. Cut the tail wire off at the proper length and taper the end if necessary. Wrap the tail wire with cotton or tow to build it up to the proper size. This wrapping should be very firm and bound tightly with lightweight thread.

MAKING THE ARTIFICIAL HEAD

The artificial head can be made in several ways. It can be carved of balsa wood, made of plaster, or you can clean the natural skull and use it. Balsa wood is preferable in many ways because it is light, strong, and will receive pins readily. If it is not convenient to use this, however, a plaster skull can be made as follows.

Mix a little molding or casting plaster to a rather thick consistency and pour it into a small cardboard box. Lay the natural head, side down, in the soft plaster with the rear of the head near one side of the box. The head should be half buried in the plaster. When the plaster has set up hard, grease the surface with stearine or petroleum jelly and cover the exposed half of the head with plaster. When this has hardened, tear away the box and separate the two halves of the mold. Remove the head and cut a matching groove on each half of the mold from the back of the head to the edge of the mold. See Fig. 20.

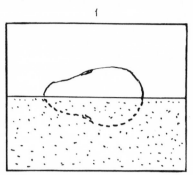

Fill box half full of plaster
and imbed half of head.

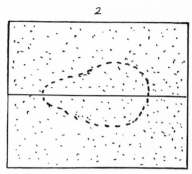

Shellac and grease top of
plaster and finish filling.

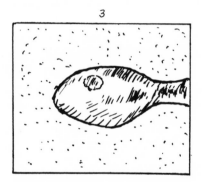

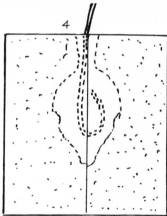

Shellac and grease inside
of mold. Place wire inside
as shown. Fill with plaster.

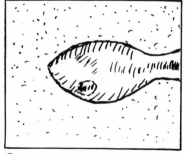

Separate mold, remove head
and cut matching groove on
both pieces from back of
head to edge of mold.

FIG. 20 Steps in making a mold of a small
mammal's head if a plaster skull is to be
used.

Shellac and grease the inside of the mold, and lay a wire in the groove with a loop bent in the head area. Put the two pieces of the mold together, then fill it with plaster through the hole alongside the wire. When this plaster sets up, you will have a plaster reproduction of the head with a wire protruding by which you can attach the head to the artificial body. The mold can be labeled and saved. It can be used over and over again when you need another head of the same kind and size.

The eye cavities should be reamed out somewhat on the plaster head to give plenty of room for the glass eyes to be set later.

If you prefer to use the natural skull instead of the balsa wood or plaster, you must clean it of all flesh and remove the brain. Run a wire through the brain cavity, and either anchor it in the skull or bend a small loop in the end which is in the brain cavity and fill the cavity with plaster to hold it. The other end of the wire is sharpened and run through the artificial body. The muscles of the skull are replaced with cotton or tow and wrapped with string. The points where the leg wires are to enter the body should be marked with an ink spot. When the artificial body is finished and ready to be put into the skin, it should look somewhat like the ermine body shown in Fig. 19.

MOUNTING

Remove the skin from the pickle bath and squeeze out the excess liquid. Inspect the skin to see if it needs any additional fleshing. The pickle will put the skin in such a condition that any bits of flesh remaining can be easily removed.

The skin may be a little stiff as it comes from the pickle, so pull and stretch it a little to relax the fibers. Rinse it in plain water, squeeze out as much as possible, and then put it in borax water for a few minutes.

When the skin is taken from the borax water, squeeze it out again, and then work it in a quantity of dry borax to help dry and fluff the fur. Shake and blow as much borax as possible out of the fur, and you are then ready to proceed with the mounting.

Sharpen one end of four wires for the legs. Run the sharpened end of a wire into the bottom of each foot and up alongside the leg bones. Wrap the bone and wire with cotton or tow to replace the leg muscles and wind with string.

When the legs are built up to the correct size, you are ready to insert the artificial body. Place the body inside the skin and insert the leg wires at the ink spots you made previously. Bend hooks in the sharp ends of the wires and anchor them in the body. Up to this point the wires should not have been bent.

Push the ends of the leg bones up firmly against the body, and fit the skin around the body to see if it fits properly. A little additional filling is usually needed around the upper part of the legs where they come in contact with the body.

Sew up the incision, starting from the rear. Insert the needle from the inside on each stitch so as not to pull fur through with the thread. If the skin seems too loose, you can put in a little additional stuffing as you go, but be careful to spread it evenly so it will not be lumpy.

When the incision has been sewed up, you can shape the legs into the proper position. Fill out the feet with a little papier mâché or water putty if needed, and sew up the incisions on the bottom of the feet.

You can now mount the animal on either a temporary or a permanent base by boring holes in the base to receive the leg wires. Be sure that the holes are spaced so that the feet will be the right distance apart and in the correct position. When this is accomplished, spread the toes in a natural position, and place pins to hold them there until they are dry. Also, bend the tail into a natural position.

When you are satisfied with the position of the body, turn your attention to the head. Work a little papier mâché or water putty into the head skin through the mouth opening. Arrange the head skin so the ears and eyes are in the right position on the skull. A little additional papier mâché or putty will probably be needed in the nose area and in the cheeks. Arrange the lips so they fit properly, and hold them in place with pins which are driven or pushed through the lips into the artificial skull. At this point you will see why the balsa-wood skull is superior to the other types.

Work some little balls of papier mâché or water putty through the eye openings and set the glass eyes. When both eyes have been installed, look at them from all angles and make sure that they are the same depth in the head and are looking in the right direction.

Clean off any papier mâché or putty that you might have gotten on the fur. If the fur is still damp, you can blow more moisture out of it with an air compressor and make it dry faster.

The ears of small animals can be held erect and in place with small pieces of cardboard placed on both the front and back of the ear and held in place with pins or paper clips. If this is not done the ears are likely to shrivel and curl in drying.

After the specimen is completely dry, remove all pins and touch up any fleshy parts that may need it with paints or stains as you were instructed to do on birds.

The main disadvantage in mounting pickled skins is that there is much more shrinkage in pickled skins than in tanned ones. This shrinkage is not as severe in small mammal skins as in large ones; but when the specimen is dry, you may find that the lips have shrunk apart slightly, and there may also be a little crack around the eyes. These blemishes can usually be corrected satisfactorily with a little modeling wax, Formula #4. If you want to give such areas as the nose and eyelids a moist appearance, they can be touched up with clear shellac, varnish, or clear gloss lacquer.

4

Skinning Game Heads and Large Mammals

A game animal should never be cut on the throat in skinning. This is especially true of all hoofed animals of either sex, whether they have horns or antlers or not. It is also true of most other animals of which a wall head mount is to be made.

With modern hunting ammunition, the practice of bleeding game is not only unnecessary, it causes the taxidermists a lot of grief. Since we usually have no control over the situation, however, we have to take the skin as it comes and do the best we can with it.

Before skinning a game head there are several measurements that should be taken. Measure the distance from the forward corner of the eye to the end of the nose, and from the end of the nose to the back of the head. These measurements will be needed whether you buy your head forms or make your own. A pair of calipers is the most accurate tool with which to make these measurements.

In the case of deer or other antlered animals, it is also helpful to measure the distance from the tip of each antler to the end of the nose. This will enable you to put the antlers on the head form in exactly the right position. You will also need to measure the circumference of the neck just behind the head, but this measurement should be taken after the skin has been removed. Fig. 21 shows where all the above measurements should be taken.

Although it is seldom done, it is a good practice to measure with your calipers the distance between the outside of the eyeballs. This can prevent the chance of your getting the glass eyes too deep or too far apart.

To skin the head of a horned or antlered animal properly for mounting, it should be cut up the back of the neck to a point just behind and between the antlers, then out and around each antler as close to the antler as possible. See Fig. 22.

Be sure to take enough cape (neck skin) to make the kind of mount you want. If it is to be a shoulder mount, cut well back on the brisket, just in front of the front legs and on around to the high point of the back above the shoulders.

Peel the skin away from the neck on each side and skin on up to the head. Cut the ears off close to the skull. Cut and pry the skin loose from around the antlers or horns, and skin on down the head. When you reach the eyes, place your finger under the eyelid from the outside so you can tell where you are cutting and not cut the eyelids. Also cut in close to the head at the mouth and nose, and completely free the skin from the head.

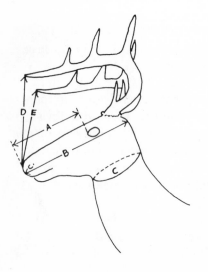

FIG. 21   Make these measurements on a game head, whether you buy forms or make your own. Neck diameter, measurement C, should be taken after the head is skinned; all other measurements should be taken before the head is skinned.

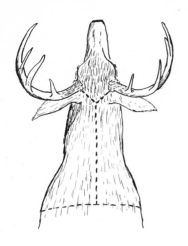

FIG. 22 The dotted lines show where to make incisions when skinning horned or antlered animals.

CUTTING OFF THE ANTLERS

The usual way of cutting off the horns or antlers of an animal is to saw from the back point of the skull through the center of the eyesockets as shown in Fig. 23. The eyeballs should be removed before doing this, as they are rather messy to saw through.

Most commercial head forms are made to fit antlers cut off in the above manner, but some are sold to fit antlers cut off as shown in Fig. 24. If you cut them off by the first method, however, they can be made to fit either type of form.

FIG. 23 The usual method of removing antlers for mounting is to saw from the back point of the skull through the middle of the eyesockets.

FIG. 24   Another method of sawing off antlers. Some commercially made forms are made to receive antlers cut off in this manner.

CARE OF EARS AND LIPS

Skin around the base of the ears until the whole butt of the ear is free from the skin. Cut all flesh from the ear butts, and separate the skin from the cartilage on the back of the ears until the ears are turned completely inside out. You might find this a little difficult to do at first, but with some practice it can be done quite easily. After the skin and cartilage have been separated for a little way in the ear, you will find it helpful to run some blunt instrument, such as the handle of a pair of pliers, down between the skin and cartilage to the tip of the ear. This opening can then be gradually enlarged. When the skin and cartilage have been separated on the back of the ear, the ear can then be turned inside out.

The cartilage will be completely removed from the ear before the head is mounted. This can be done now, but the skin on the front of the ear is quite tender and is sometimes damaged during the tanning process. For this reason, it is usually better to leave the cartilage attached to the front of the ear until the skin has been tanned, especially if the skin is to be sent to a commercial tannery.

After the ears have been taken care of, give your attention to the

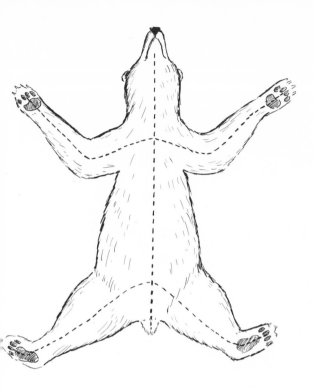

lips. The lip skin must be split between the inside and outside skin. The cartilage between the nostrils should also be split, and any excess flesh from the entire nose and mouth area removed. After this is done, the skin should be heavily salted.

SKINNING FOR WHOLE MOUNTS AND RUGS

If an animal is being skinned for a whole mount or a rug, the body incisions are usually made as shown in Fig. 25.

Hornless animals such as cats and bears need not be cut on the back of the neck when being skinned for a whole mount or rug, but a doe deer should be because it is almost impossible to sew up the throat of a deer without the seam showing.

Hoofed animals to be mounted whole should be disjointed at the lowest joint of the leg. This joint is right down in the base of the hoof, not above the hoof. Most taxidermists leave the hoof attached to the skin, but in museum work the skin is usually separated from the hoof and only the outer shell of the hoof is used in the mount.

Animals with pads or paws may be cut down through the center of the pad or paw and disjointed at the forward joint of the toes, leaving the claws attached to the skin.

Free the skin from the body and legs first and then from the head. After the skin has been completely removed from the body, do any fleshing that is necessary, and attend to the ears and lips as already described.

Spread the skin out in a cool, shady place, flesh side up, and apply salt heavily to all parts. The salt will draw moisture out of the skin; therefore, it should be placed on a slant if possible, so the water can drain off. The water should never be allowed to stand in puddles on the skin.

After the hide has been salted for a day or two, any additional fleshing that may be needed can be done more easily than when the hide was fresh. After fleshing, apply more salt. When the skin has finished draining, but before it is completely dry, it may be folded or rolled up until it is ready to be tanned.

SEAMLESS-LEG SKINNING

Another method of skinning, devised by the late Carl Akeley, is the seamless-leg method. This method was used by Mr. Akeley on almost all of his large mammal work. It is much more difficult and time-consuming than the usual method of splitting the legs. For this reason, it is seldom used, but it should be used on all short-haired mammals if the highest degree of perfection is to be attained.

In this method the belly incision and the back-of-the-neck incision are made in the usual way. The only incisions made on the legs are from the hoof up to the dewclaws and around the top of the hoof.

The legs must be disjointed from the body and pulled out of the leg skin by turning the leg skin wrong side out.

Animals skinned by this method must be mounted on a manikin with detachable legs. Directions for making such a manikin are given in Chapter 7.

5

Tanning

In years past, it was the usual practice to pickle all mammal skins in a salt-and-alum or a salt-and-sulfuric acid solution before mounting. Many taxidermists still use this method today because it is quicker and cheaper than tanning, but it is also inferior. Pickling is a small part of the tanning process. It removes the glue from the hide and preserves the skin to some extent, but it does not convert the skin into soft leather. A skin which has been pickled dries hard and stiff and usually shrinks so much that the muscular detail in the mounted animal is lost. Also, the stitches almost invariably pull out, leaving a space of half an inch or more where the incisions were sewed up. This is especially true in heavy hides.

There are dozens of chemicals and processes that are used in tanning. There is, however, no magic formula by which a raw skin can be converted into soft, pliable leather without a lot of hard work.

Several methods will be given here by which skins may be tanned at home by hand. The novice should be forewarned, though, that hand tanning is a laborious and time-consuming job, and one cannot expect to achieve results comparable to those attained by a well-equipped tannery. If you turn out a reasonably satisfactory job in your first few attempts you are lucky.

Most taxidermists will fare much better by sending their hides to a reputable tannery which does work for the taxidermy trade.

PREPARING THE SKIN

The first and one of the most important steps in any tanning process is to prepare the skin properly before the actual tanning is started. Failure to do this is probably responsible for more disappointments in tanning than any other error.

Every trace of fat and flesh must be removed, and on heavy hides, part of the skin itself must be shaved down.

It is very difficult to flesh and shave down a freshly skinned hide. A skin which has been salted for a few days, but is not dry, is usually in the proper condition for being shaved down.

If the skin has dried hard and stiff, it must be soaked in water until it is soft again. The length of time required for soaking will, of course, depend upon the thickness and dryness of the skin. You should inspect the skin often during soaking. After it begins to soften, take it out of the water occasionally and trim down the hard areas so they will absorb water more easily. The softening can be speeded up somewhat by adding a little borax and soap to the water.

When the skin is soft, take it out of the water and let it drain, but not dry. Lay it over a smooth beam, flesh side up, and shave down any thick, hard spots. If the hard, dense spots still persist, they should be wet again and worked over the beam until soft. Skins should not be left in the water any longer than necessary, for the hair might start slipping.

Fig. 26 shows three ways a shaving beam can be made. The one on the left can be folded against the wall when not in use. The middle one can be moved around, but takes up quite a bit of floor space. The small one on the right can be clamped or nailed to a tabletop whenever needed; it is handy for small skins or for working on the heads of larger skins.

The shaving down of a skin can be done with a sharp knife, but a currier's knife, Fig. 27, is made for the purpose and does the job

FIG. 26   Three types of homemade shaving beams. The one on the left can be folded against the wall when not in use. The small one nailed to the work table is handy for smaller skins and for turning the ears of larger animals.

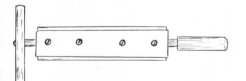

FIG. 27   A currier's knife. It holds two very sharp replaceable blades with turned edges. It is almost indispensable for shaving down heavy hides before tanning them.

much faster and with less danger of cutting holes in the skin. This knife has a removable blade on each side. These blades have the sharp edge turned at a right angle to the rest of the blade, and if you use it correctly, you can shave down a skin much more evenly than you could with any other knife.

Skins which are very greasy should be given a quick bath in white gasoline and allowed to drain.

When there are no more hard spots in the skin, and it has been shaved down to a uniform thickness, it should be ready for tanning.

The above instructions apply to all skins, except that skins with very fine fur should not be soaked in water or any other liquid as this sometimes causes the hair to mat badly. These skins are best softened by applying water or a wet cloth to the flesh side and keeping it wet until the skin is thoroughly relaxed. These skins should be tanned by applying the tanning liquor to the flesh side in the form of a paste or liquid. Other skins with coarser fur or hair may safely be submerged and soaked in the tanning solution.

From the following instructions, pick the method that seems most applicable to the skin you are working on.

Since the drying and finishing process is the same regardless of the tanning method used, the tanning methods will be described first and then the finishing process which applies to all methods.

When the skin is immersed in the tanning solution it should be allowed to stay from one day to a week or more, depending upon the thickness of the skin and the temperature of the solution. The solution should be kept at normal room temperature if possible. Examine the skin at intervals to see if it has turned white on the flesh side. If it has, make a small cut in the thickest part. If it is white all the way through it is ready to be taken out; otherwise, let it soak longer. It is better to leave the skin in the solution longer than necessary than to take it out too soon.

If you use the paste method, tack the skin out on a smooth, horizontal surface and apply the paste evenly to the flesh side in a coat about one-eighth of an inch thick. The next day, scrap off most of the paste and apply another coat. A rather heavy skin may need a third application, but two coats are usually enough on small skins.

Allow the last coat to stay on the skin for three or four days.

Scrape off the final coat of paste, remove the tacks, and wash the skin in a water-borax solution, mixed one ounce of borax to each gallon. Finally rinse in plain water, and proceed according to the directions for finishing.

If you prefer to paint the tanning solution on the skin without making it into a paste, you should sprinkle sawdust on the skin to keep the tanning liquor from forming puddles. The skin should also be covered with a cloth dampened with the tanning liquor.

Applications should be made about six to eight hours apart until three or four applications have been made. After the last application has been on the skin for six or eight hours, rinse the skin thoroughly in plain water. Squeeze out as much water as possible, but do not wring the skin. Spread the skin out, flesh side up, and allow it to almost dry; then wash it in a water-borax solution, again mixed an ounce of borax to each gallon. Finally rinse in plain water and proceed with the finishing.

Following are several formulas which can be used:

Salt and alum formula for painting or paste application: Dissolve 1 pound of alum in 1 gallon of soft water. In another container, dissolve 4 ounces of washing soda (sal soda) and ½ pound of salt in ½ gallon of soft water. When dissolved, slowly add the soda and salt solution to the alum solution while stirring constantly. Use this solution in liquid form or mix with bran or flour as needed to make a thin paste.

Salt and alum formula for immersing skins: Dissolve 2 pounds of salt and 1 pound of alum in 4 gallons of soft water. Soak the prepared skin in this solution until it is white all the way through. Stir the skin around in the solution several times each day. When the skin is white all the way through, remove it from the solution and wash as described above; it is then ready for the finishing process.

Salt and sulfuric acid formula: Skins may be soaked in this solution or it may be applied to the flesh side in a paste or liquid form. Into 2 gallons of soft water, dissolve 2 pounds of salt. When the salt has dissolved, slowly add 1 ounce (by measure) of sulfuric acid while stirring the solution constantly.

CAUTION: *Use extreme care when using sulfuric acid. If it comes in contact with your skin it can cause severe burns. When pouring it into the salt solution, avoid breathing the fumes.*

Soak or treat the skins with this solution until they are white all the way through just as in the methods above. After tanning skins in a sulfuric acid solution, they should be washed thoroughly in water to which a handful of ordinary baking soda has been added per gallon. This will neutralize the acid. After that they should be washed in plain water; then you can proceed with the finishing process.

Aluminum sulfate tannage: This formula consists of a combination of mineral and vegetable products. It produces leather of more durable quality than the acid tan and softer leather than the alum tan. Also, it does not shrink the skins as much as alum. The solution is made as follows: In 1½ gallons of warm, soft water, dissolve 1 pound of salt and 1 pound of (iron-free) aluminum sulfate. In another container, dissolve 3 ounces of gambier or terra japonica in 1 quart of boiling water. Mix the two solutions together and add enough water to make 2 gallons of liquid.

Put the skins in this solution after it has cooled or treat the flesh side with the liquid or paste as previously described. When tanned, wash the skin in water to which 1 ounce of borax has been added per gallon, and then in plain water. After this, proceed with the finishing process.

FINISHING

After the final washing of the skin, squeeze out as much water as you can and stretch the skin out, flesh side up.

Mix a thin, sudsy paste of good laundry soap (not detergent) and apply a thin coat of this to the flesh side of the skin. Allow the soap to soak in overnight; then apply a thin coat of warm neat's-foot oil or melted butter. (If the skin was originally very greasy, this oiling may not be necessary.)

Allow the skin to dry until it begins to shrink and turn dark, but is not completely dry. Test the skin occasionally by stretching a small area from side to side. If it turns white where stretched, it is ready for the next step. (Some people like to let the skin dry completely and then cover it with a wet cloth until it is at the stretch-and-turn-white stage described above. Either way works equally well.)

Pull and stretch the skin in all directions. Draw it back and forth across the edge of a board in a shoe-shining motion or pull it back and forth through a metal ring suspended from the ceiling or wall. This working of the skin should continue until it is dry and soft. This is one of the most important parts of the tanning process. Even if everything else was done correctly, the skin will dry hard and stiff if this important step is not done.

If the skin still dries hard in spots, these areas should be moistened again until soft and the operation repeated.

If the skin seems too oily when finished, it can be given a quick bath in white gasoline and dried by working in hardwood sawdust or cornmeal.

Commercial tanneries are equipped with large motor-driven drums which are partially filled with hardwood sawdust. The skins are tumbled in these drums at intervals during the drying process. This not only helps to dry and soften the skin, it also helps to brighten the fur.

The cost of a sawdust tumbler would be prohibitive unless you plan to go into the tanning business, but there are other tanning tools that you can buy or make which will make the job of breaking up a tanned hide a little easier. Fig. 28 shows three types of stakers which are useful in breaking up the fibers of a skin in the finishing

FIG. 28   A staking rack and three types of staking tools. The rack holds the hide firmly. The tools have dull metal blades which are scraped over the hide with considerable force to help soften and break up the fibers during the tanning process.

operation. All of these have a rounded steel blade which is not sharp but is intended to apply stretching pressure to the skin.

MAKING BUCKSKIN

To make buckskin from the hides of deer or other animals, it is first necessary to remove the hair. After the skin has been fleshed and prepared for tanning as previously described, soak it in lime water. To make the lime water, mix 1 pound of hydrated lime in a small amount of water to form a paste. Add enough water to this to make 4 gallons of solution, and mix well.

Put the skin in this solution and weight it down so that all parts are covered. Stir the hide in the solution three or four times each day.

When the hair is completely loose, which will usually take from one to two weeks, remove the skin. Put the skin over a smooth beam, flesh side down, and with a dull knife or other blade, scrape off the hair. If the hair does not come off easily and cleanly, put it back in the lime water awhile longer.

When the hair has been removed, wash the skin thoroughly in warm water to remove as much of the lime as possible. The skin must then be soaked for about a day in a boric acid solution to neutralize any remaining lime. To make the boric acid solution, dissolve 4 ounces of boric acid in 4 gallons of water.

After the skin is removed from this solution, wash it through several changes of plain water, let it drain, and then it may be tanned by any of the methods already described.

CAUTION: Never mix or keep tanning solutions in metal containers. The chemicals will attack or corrode the metal. Always use wood, crockery, or heavy plastic containers.

6

Modeling and Mold Making

Many taxidermists today depend largely upon commercially made forms or manikins for almost all their mounts. A large selection of forms is now available from taxidermy supply houses. Some of these are excellent, while others are almost worthless, and it would be impossible to turn out a first-class mount on them without doing some altering. One should never be fooled into thinking that just because a form is sold commercially it is anatomically correct.

In museum taxidermy, individual models are usually made for each animal to be mounted, and the mold is used only once. This would, of course, be impractical and impossible for the commercial taxidermist; but he should at least know how it is done and be able to do it if the need arises. There are many times when a taxidermist gets specimens for mounting for which no commercially made form is available. In such cases you have to make your own forms or turn the job down.

Your spare time, or slow seasons, can be profitably spent in making models, molds, and forms for specimens you are likely to get in your area. This is especially true of head forms. The game heads you get in for mounting in any given year will very likely be duplicated many times in the following years. If you accumulate a collection of molds, they can be used over and over again for many years. There is a great satisfaction in using your creative ability in modeling forms. In the long run, it will not only save you money, but will give your work a certain individual distinction.

When you acquire a specimen for which you wish to make a model and mold, the first step is to make certain careful and exact measurements of the body, some before and some after skinning. Fig. 29 shows some of the more important measurements to take, but do not necessarily limit your measurements to these. Take any measurements that you think might be a help to you later. Sketches and photographs should also be made of the muscle structure and any other characteristics that may be important.

FIG. 29   Field measurements that should be taken on the carcass of an animal to be mounted whole. Don't limit your measurements to these, however; when you're modeling a large animal you can never have too many measurements.

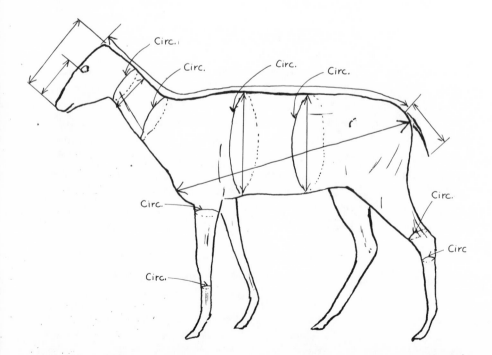

After all measurements and sketches have been made, cut the flesh off the bones and save the complete skeleton. If you are in camp, the roughed-out skeleton can be tied in a bundle and allowed to dry. It should, however, be hung from a tree limb or kept in a place where dogs or other animals cannot get to it.

Later, the roughed-out skeleton can be soaked in water or even boiled for a short time to make it easier to clean; but be careful not to boil it long enough to make the joints come apart. The bones need not be perfectly clean, as they will not be used in the finished animal.

Next, decide on the position you want to make the model. Set the skeleton up in the desired position as shown in Fig. 30. The legs are held in place by strong wires or iron rods which are tied securely to the bones and attached to the center board and the

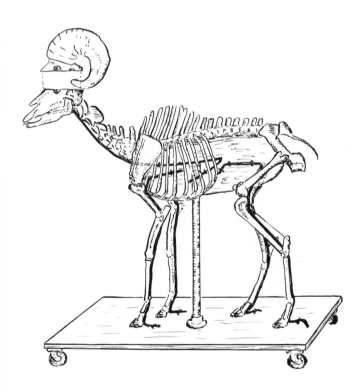

FIG. 30 A skeleton, or armature, set up for making a life-size clay model.

base. The head and neck are also supported by a rod attached to the center board.

If you wish, you can use only the skull and leg bones as shown in Fig. 31, but there is less chance of making errors if you use the entire skeleton.

The more fleshy portions of the body may be partially filled in by covering over the skeleton with wire netting or hardware cloth. See Fig. 32. This can be strengthened by dipping strips of burlap in plaster and placing it over the wire netting to form a hard base for the modeling clay. If you find later that the wire netting sticks out a little too far in places, it can be pounded in with a hammer and no harm is done.

A hole should be drilled through the heelbone of each hind leg. A wire is attached through this hole and the other end is attached to the thighbone. See Fig. 32. This wire represents the Achilles tendon. It may be wrapped with sisal or some other material to make it better support the clay.

When the rough form is finished, use ordinary water clay and model the body according to your sketches and measurements. Sometimes it is better to model the head and lower legs with an oil-base permanent-type modeling composition. The clay is so thin on these areas that water clay sometimes dries and starts falling off before the model is finished.

When modeling any kind of figure, always build up the bulk of the form before you start trying to put in too much detail. Imagine how the live animal would look with the hair shaved off. This is about the way your model should look when finished.

When you have the clay model finished to the right proportions, use a paintbrush dipped in water and smooth the surface nicely.

Always keep the clay model covered with wet cloths when you are not working on it. When left overnight or longer, the model should be wrapped in wet cloth and then covered with plastic sheeting.

MODELING TOOLS

The human hand is the best modeling tool there is, as any sculptor will tell you. There are dozens of different shapes and sizes of modeling tools on the market which look pretty and can possibly be

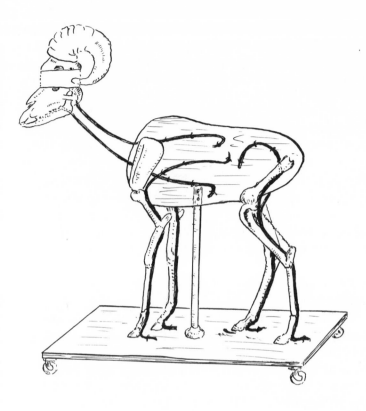

FIG. 31   Instead of using the entire skeleton, you can use just the leg bones and skull. The body and neck portions can be roughly shaped with hardware cloth or wire netting and covered with burlap or sisal dipped in plaster. This eliminates the need for so much clay.

FIG. 32   Wire netting is shaped over the more fleshy parts of the body before modeling with clay.

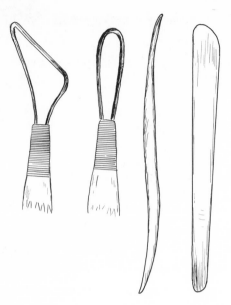

used at some time or other, but very few of them are really necessary. Fig. 33 shows a few types that will be most useful in most modeling jobs.

MAKING THE MOLD

The plaster mold of a whole animal which you expect to use more than one time must be made in several sections so it can be removed from the model, and so the cast or manikin to be made inside can be removed without breaking the mold.

The mold separations can be accomplished by making one section at a time. This is done by first deciding where the lines of separation should be, and then putting a wall along these lines on the clay model. The easiest way is to cut strips of thin brass or other metal about an inch wide and sticking them into the clay model to form a wall. Another way is to roll out pieces of clay on a smooth surface, making a sort of a clay rope. Flatten the clay out and trim both edges, thereby making a strip about an inch wide. These strips are laid edgewise on the clay model and pressed down to hold them in place. A combination of these two methods can often be used to advantage because in some places the clay on the model will be too thin to hold the metal strips. Fig. 34 shows approximately how the strips should be placed on a four-legged animal in a standing position.

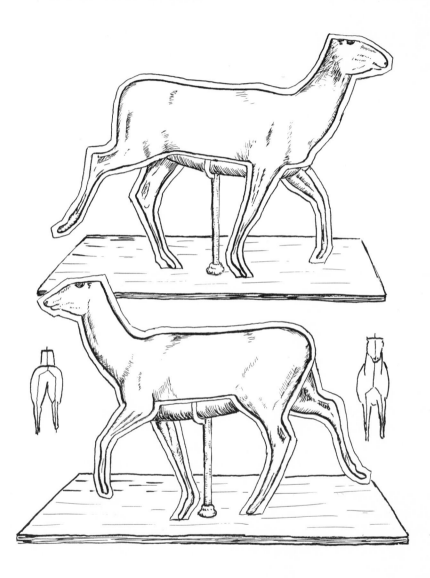

FIG. 34 A finished clay model, showing the approximate position of the brass or clay walls that will separate the sections of the mold.

When the partition strips are in place, you can proceed with the making of the mold. Mix a quantity of molding plaster or hydrocal to a creamy consistency. Dip your hand in the plaster and apply a coat of plaster over one section of the model. This coat can be quite thin, but be sure the whole area is covered. When this coat begins to set up, dip pieces of burlap or wads of sisal in plaster and apply this over the whole area. Continue to do this until the mold is about an inch thick.

When the first section of the mold has hardened, remove the wall between it and the next section to be done. Cut several notches in the edge of the hardened mold so the next section will always fit exactly in place. Give the edge of the mold a coat of shellac, and when this is dry, apply a coat of stearine so the second section will not stick to the first.

Make the other sections of the mold in the same manner until the whole model is covered.

On large molds, the larger sections should be reinforced with iron rods, pieces of pipe, or strong pieces of wood. These can be laid against the outer surface of the mold and attached in several places with strips of burlap dipped in plaster. This will greatly strengthen the mold and make it easier to remove it from the model without breaking it. It also helps to prevent warpage in the mold. Fig. 35 shows reinforcement rods on a mold.

It is best to leave the mold on the model for several hours, as it will continue to harden for some time. After it is completely hard, you can remove the mold by carefully prying the sections apart. To take out the underneath sections you will have to pull the legs of the model out of the way after the side sections have been removed.

With the separating walls placed as shown in Fig. 34, the mold will be in four pieces. If you wish, you could put another divider down the center of the belly and make the mold in six pieces, or you can saw the two bottom sections in half after the mold is taken off.

After the mold has been removed, wash off the film of clay inside, and patch any large bubble holes. Tie the pieces of the mold together and let it dry thoroughly. When it is dry, which will take several days, give the inside at least one coat of shellac. A coat of stearine is then applied before each use.

The above method is generally used in museum work by highly

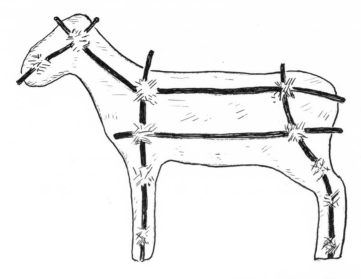

FIG. 35   The outside of one section of a plaster mold, showing rods used for reinforcement.

skilled craftsmen. Until you have had considerable experience in modeling and making molds of smaller objects it would not be advisable to attempt this on a large animal.

MAKING DEATH MASKS

A death mask, or study mask, is nothing more than a reproduction of part of the head of an animal before it is skinned. In the modeling of head forms, and in the actual mounting of heads, it is often very helpful to have some death masks of various animals in your shop for reference. They are quite easy to make.

When you get a fresh head that you would like to make a mask of, wash any blood or other foreign matter from the head, and arrange the mouth and lips in a natural position.

Mix up some thick lather of soap and water and apply this over the area you want to make the mold of. Be sure the hair is well saturated with the lather. (Instead of soap lather you can use a thin mixture of clay and water.)

Mix some molding or casting plaster to the consistency of thick batter and spread this over the area you wish to reproduce. Do not rub the plaster into the hair too much, just spread it on the surface. When the first coat begins to harden, apply another coat until the mold is about half an inch thick. Do not reinforce this mold with anything; just use plaster.

When the mold has set up hard, gently pull it off the head. The soap or clay will keep it from sticking to the hair.

You can now paint the inside of the mold with the soapy lather, clay wash, or stearine and fill it with plaster. When this has thoroughly hardened, chip or break the mold off and you will have a reproduction of the animal's face. A mask of this type is usually made of only the nose and front part of the head. If you try to take in too much of the head you might run into trouble in getting the mold off unless you make it in pieces. Fig. 36 shows death masks of an elk, deer, bear, and wolverine.

MODELING WALL HEADS

Modeling for wall head mounts is not very difficult if you have a skull to model over and a few measurements to guide you. Suppose you want to make a model for a deer head form. About all you will need in the way of equipment is the deer's skull, a piece of 2x4-inch lumber, a few nails or screws, and some clay.

If it is going to be a model for a straight-front upright shoulder mount, you should first make an outline sketch on paper. Draw a rough outline profile of the head and neck as far back as you want

FIG. 36   Death masks of elk, deer, black bear, and wolverine. These can be a great help when modeling head forms.

the model to be. Lay a piece of 2x4 on the neck outline, and saw one end to fit against the skull at the proper angle. The other end should be sawed to fit against the wall or backboard. See Fig. 37. If the 2x4 needs to be notched somewhere to allow for the curve in the neck, you can do so.

Attach the skull to the 2x4 securely with wires. Attach the other end of the 2x4 to a backboard that is larger than the back of the model will be. It is usually necessary to attach some little "butter-flies" to the 2x4 as shown in Fig. 37 to help support the clay.

You can now model the head, using the measurements you should have made earlier as a guide. If you have a death mask as described above, it will be a help when modeling the nose and mouth.

When your model is complete, you can make a mold as described earlier. A head mold can usually be made in only two pieces, and it will last for years if properly taken care of.

It is a good practice to write in bold letters on the side of each mold what it is, and three basic measurements, such as "W/T Deer—St.Fr.Sh. 7½—13—18." The three figures represent the nose-to-eye, nose-to-back-of-head, and circumference-of-neck measurements. Later, when you have a collection of molds, this will enable you to find the kind and size you are looking for.

If the model is to have a sharply turned neck, or is in some position in which you cannot use a straight piece of wood in the neck, you can use iron rods instead of wood. The rods may be covered with wire netting or hardware cloth, which is in turn covered with a layer of plaster and burlap. This will greatly reduce the amount of clay that is needed. See Fig. 38.

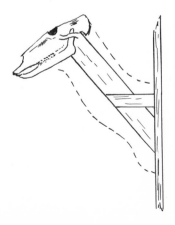

FIG. 37   One method of setting up a skull for modeling a head form, using a braced 2×4 for support.

FIG. 38   Another method of setting up a skull, using an iron rod and wire netting. This method may be necessary if there is a sharp turn in the neck.

MODELING RUG HEAD FORMS

Modeling rug head forms is quite simple, although a little distortion is required to give the proper effect. Since the skin does not go all the way around a rug head form, it is made somewhat wider at the bottom.

The model can be made over the natural skull, and it may have the mouth either open or closed. Most rugs are made with open mouths, but some people prefer closed-mouth rugs.

Fig. 39 shows a bear and bobcat skull with rug forms which were made from models and molds made over these skulls. This will give you some idea as to the distortion that must be made in a rug form; otherwise, the rug will have a tendency to look shrivel-headed.

A mold for a rug head is made in two pieces, separated down the center. When the first half of the mold has hardened, it should have two or three notches cut in the edge so the other half will always fit exactly in place without slipping.

Since the top of the mold is more or less rounded, it is also helpful to make a "mother mold" over part of the two halves of the original mold. The mother mold should be made flat on top so that when you turn the whole thing over to make a form inside, the flat surface of the mother mold will rest squarely on the table and keep the mold from rocking around. It also holds the two pieces of the head mold together, eliminating the necessity for tying them.

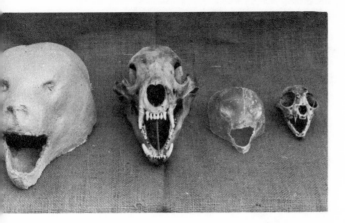

FIG. 39   Bear and bobcat rug head forms and the skulls which were used to make the original models. The bear head is made of plaster and burlap, the bobcat head of fiberglass.

MAKING MOTHER MOLDS

As stated above, a mother mold is a mold made over two or more pieces of another mold to hold them securely together while making a cast or form inside.

To make a mother mold over a rug head mold you simply smooth off the top surface of the head mold as much as possible. Build a clay wall around the area to be covered by the mother mold, and fill this area with plaster, which should be reinforced to make it as strong as possible. See Fig. 40.

This mother-mold system will be found convenient and useful in many other instances when using a mold which is made in several pieces. For example, suppose you want to make a mold of an object such as the model of the squirrel shown in Fig. 41. Obviously, you could not make a mold of this in two pieces without destroying the model when taking the mold off. Furthermore, if you did this, you could not take a cast from the mold without destroying either the mold or the cast in the process.

The answer, then, is to make a mold in as many pieces as necessary so that it can be taken off without damage to the model or the mold. See Fig. 42.

Before the pieces of the mold are removed from the model, the outside should be smoothed as much as possible, then shellacked and greased with stearine. A mother mold is then made in as few

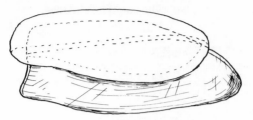

Mother mold over rug head mold

FIG. 40 Making a "mother mold" over a mold for a rug head form. Mother molds are useful over many types of plaster piece molds to hold the pieces together.

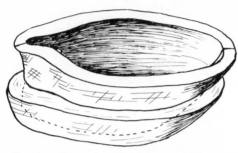

Rug head mold resting in mother mold

FIG. 41 Clay model of a squirrel over which a plaster piece mold is to be made.

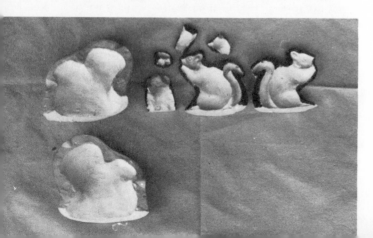

FIG. 42 Plaster piece mold and mother mold made over the clay model shown in Fig. 41.

pieces as possible over the inner mold. In Fig. 42, the two large pieces are the mother mold and the smaller pieces are the inner mold. From a mold such as this you can make a large number of casts.

MAKING RUBBER MOLDS

Sometimes you may wish to make many reproductions of an object of which a plaster mold would not be practical. In such cases, a rubber mold is often the answer.

You can buy liquid latex from an art supply dealer or he can get it for you. It is often used for making plaques or other objects which have projections forming undercuts which would make a hard plaster mold impractical. Rubber molds are also very useful to the taxidermist for casting artificial teeth and tongues as described in Chapter 11.

To make a rubber mold, the liquid latex or rubber is painted or smeared over the object and allowed to dry. When the first coat is thoroughly dry, apply another coat; continue to do this until the mold is thick enough to be durable. Usually you can apply from one to two coats per day, depending upon drying conditions. Ordinarily, five or six coats will be enough, depending upon the size and shape of the mold you are making. These molds are tough, but quite flexible, and sometimes it may be desirable to back them with a plaster mold to support the rubber when making a cast.

MAKING MOLDS
WITH DENTAL IMPRESSION MATERIAL

Sometimes it is desirable to make a quick, flexible mold of some object such as the comb of a chicken or the inside of an animal's mouth. To make a rubber mold would take far too long, and a plaster mold would not be practical. In such cases, dental impression material is very useful. It is made in several forms, but the powder form is generally best for taxidermy work.

The powder is mixed with water according to the directions of the manufacturer, and quickly applied to the area to be reproduced. It sets up in two or three minutes to a tough rubbery consistency. Because of the high water content in this material, it shrinks quite rapidly. Your casts, therefore, should be made from such a mold within a few hours if accuracy is important.

MAKING A MOLD OVER A CARCASS

Instead of setting up the skeleton and making a clay model of a whole animal as described earlier in this chapter, many taxidermists make a mold directly over the carcass of the animal whenever possible. This is not always easy, but it requires considerably less skill than the clay-model method, and the results are likely to be more satisfactory unless you are quite adept at modeling and know your anatomy.

The biggest problem in making a mold over a carcass is in placing the carcass in the right position and keeping it there while you make the mold. On an animal the size of a fox or bobcat it is not too difficult usually, but the larger the animal the more difficult it becomes.

To begin with, the animal should be carefully skinned so that the surface muscles are not all hacked up and rough. The belly should be split down the center and all the viscera removed. Wipe out the body cavity to remove any blood or other fluids that may be present.

Cut a piece of board to fit inside the body cavity as shown in Fig. 43. Somewhere along the middle of this board, nail another narrow board at right angles to it. This latter board will be a center support.

With the board in place inside the body cavity, fill the cavity with excelsior or some other light material to give the abdomen the right shape. Then sew up the incision.

Cut off the support board to make the animal stand at the correct height, then securely attach the center support to the base. Run wires up through the flesh of the legs to make them stay in position better, and arrange the legs in the desired position. Hold the feet in place on the base with tacks or small nails. Run a stiff wire into the nostril area, through the head and neck, and into the body.

When you have the body arranged in the position you want, you should inject a formaldehyde solution into all the fleshy areas of the body. This will harden the muscles somewhat and help to prevent them from sagging.

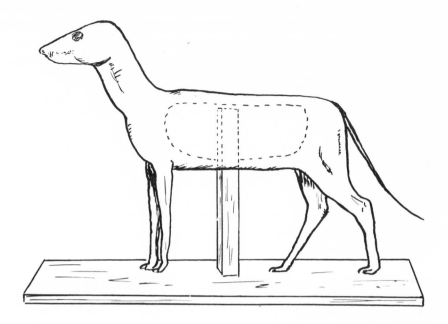

FIG. 43 When making a mold over the carcass of an animal, use a center board inside the carcass to support the body. The head must also be held in position, either by supporting it from underneath or by running stiff wires down through the mouth and neck and attaching them to the center board in the body.

The eyeballs should be removed if you have not done so already. The eyesockets may be filled with clay and slightly pushed down into a concave shape.

If you want to make the form with the mouth open, you should open the mouth as wide as you want it and fill it with clay to hold it there.

You can model the lips and nostrils at this time or go ahead and make the mold, and model them on the form later.

Before actually starting to make the mold, you will have to decide where the partition walls will be. Ordinarily, the sides can be made in one piece, and the underparts and inside of the legs in another piece. Since the center support will be in the way, however, it will be necessary to make the underside of the mold in two parts as shown in Fig. 34.

Since metal strips cannot be stuck into the carcass, and since a clay wall will not stick to the carcass very well either, the best way to make a separating wall in this case is to use strips of corrugated cardboard. The strips should be cut to conform to the contours of the body and should be about an inch wide. They may be held in place by sticking wires down through the holes formed by the corrugations, and into the carcass. The ends should be cut to fit flush against each other. If the ends do not want to stay together properly, you can put a piece of tape over the seam.

When the wall is in place, give it a coat of shellac; then paint the carcass and wall with stearine. The mold can then be made as described earlier.

Molds can be made on the carcass of large mammals in very much the same way, except that they usually have to be made with the body lying down. Large animals are so heavy and hard to handle that it usually takes several people to do the job. Even under the best circumstances there is a lot of guesswork, and it is very difficult to wind up with the animal standing in a natural position.

7

Making Manikins and Ear Liners

After you have the mold made of your clay model or the carcass, the next step is to make a hollow manikin or form inside the mold. This form will be a reproduction of the model, and will be used to mount the skin over.

Manikins have been made of many different materials, but the cheapest and most practical materials for the do-it-yourself taxidermist are either laminated paper or plaster-and-burlap. Each has its advantages over the other.

Most of the forms sold by taxidermy supply houses are made of laminated paper. These forms are light, strong, and usually quite satisfactory. Plaster-and-burlap forms are perhaps a little heavier, but can be made much more quickly, and are also quite satisfactory if properly made. For some reason, however, plaster-and-burlap forms are rarely, if ever, sold commercially, and many taxidermists have never heard of them.

Some commercially made forms are now being made of various kinds of plastic compositions. These are very good and sell for about the same price as paper forms. The initial cost of producing them is quite high, but after that they can probably be produced much more cheaply per unit than paper forms.

Forms can easily be made in the home shop out of fiberglass. This is much more expensive than the above-mentioned materials, but it makes a very light, almost indestructible form. For some small mounts, especially, it is well worth the extra cost. Instructions for making forms of all these materials will follow.

MAKING PAPER FORMS

A new mold should be shellacked and greased with stearine before starting to make a form. Afterward, it is only necessary to apply a thin coat of stearine before each use.

The best paper to use is ordinary unglazed red rosin building paper. It can be purchased in rolls from many builder's supply stores. The paper comes in 20- or 30-pound weight. The 20-pound paper is best for small forms and the 30-pound paper for larger forms.

There are many formulas for making paste which can be used in making paper forms. Some people prefer a rather thin paste, while others like it thicker. This is largely a matter of personal choice. With a little experience you will arrive at a formula that suits you best. Formula #9, given in the appendix, is a good basic formula and can be thickened or thinned as desired.

The paper should always be torn instead of cut. The feathered edges of torn paper overlap more smoothly and result in a much neater job.

To begin, a quantity of paper should be torn into convenient-sized pieces to work with, say 12 by 15 inches. Keep these pieces in a stack by the mold you are going to work in. The paper is usually laid in the mold in strips from 2 to 3 or 4 inches wide, depending upon the area and contour of the surface to be covered. Pieces that are too big usually have a tendency to pull out of depressions or will not lie smoothly in the first place. The strips can be torn from the larger pieces of paper as you go.

With a paintbrush, apply paste to both sides of the paper. Tear strips and lay them in the mold as shown in Fig. 44. The strips should extend beyond the edge of the mold 2 or 3 inches. These loose ends will later be folded back in to form a neat edge.

FIG. 44 When making laminated paper manikins or forms, the first layer of paper should be laid in the mold in strips, with the edges extending beyond the mold 2 or 3 inches.

When the entire surface of the mold has been covered with the first layer of paper, go over it to see that it is pressed down and makes contact with the mold in all depressions. Sometimes it is helpful to put a thin layer of papier mâché over areas such as in the nose and around the eyes where the depressions in the mold are the deepest. When the next layer of paper is pressed against this it will hold the first layer down nicely.

Keep adding layers of paper in the same manner until the form is built up thick enough. The second and each succeeding layer of paper should extend only to the edge of the mold. Only the first layer should extend beyond the edges of the mold.

If you have trouble remembering the area that has been covered by each layer and think you might wind up with thin spots in the form, you can paste a layer of newspaper between each layer of the building paper. Then there is no danger of missing any spots.

The number of layers required will, of course, depend upon the size of the form and the weight of the paper you are using. A deer head form should be at least a quarter-inch thick in the thinnest places and somewhat thicker in the nose and mouth areas and around the eyes. Larger forms such as elk and moose head forms, which might have to bear the weight of heavy antlers, should be about twice as thick.

After the final layer of paper has been installed, fold the loose ends of the first layer back over the other layers and paste them down inside the form. Be very careful that the edge of the form is even with the edge of the mold.

When all pieces of the form have been finished in this manner, lay the molds away until the paper is dry enough to hold its shape. The pieces of the form can then be carefully removed from the mold and laid on a flat surface with the edges down so they will not warp. This will allow the air to circulate on both sides of the form and make it dry more evenly.

When both sides are dry, or almost so, you can fit the pieces together and tie them securely. When this is done, take strips of paper and paste them over the seams inside. Also, paste one layer of paper over the outside seam.

If the form is for a horned or antlered animal, you should install the antler block at this time. For this you can use a piece of white pine which will take screws without splitting, or you can use a piece of three-quarter-inch waterproof plywood. Cut the block to fit inside the form opposite where the skull plate will be attached. See Fig. 45. This block can be fastened in place by gluing strips of paper over it.

Newly made paper forms will warp quite easily if subjected to any pressure while drying, or if one side is allowed to dry faster than the other. They should, therefore, never be stacked up or placed where one side will get more heat than the other.

After the forms are dry they should be given at least one good coat of shellac or lacquer before being used.

In making forms for whole animals which require an antler block, the block must be installed before the two sides of the head are put together; otherwise, you will not be able to reach into the head area to install it.

FIG. 45   Dotted line shows where antler block is located in head form.

The leg rods must also be installed before the pieces of the form are put together. These rods are bent to fit inside the legs, and should lie along the body wall for some distance to give added strength. They can be attached to the form by gluing several layers of paper over them at intervals. A double twisted tail wire should also be installed in the form before it is assembled. Fig. 46 shows the leg rods and tail wire in place in the form.

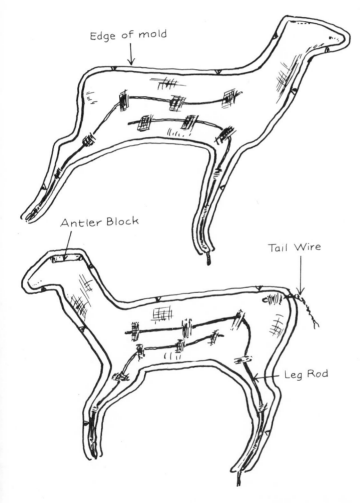

FIG. 46   Leg rods and tail wire are placed inside the form as shown.

PLASTER-AND-BURLAP MANIKINS

Plaster-and-burlap forms can be made much quicker than the paper forms described above.

Lay out the pieces of your mold and shellac the inside if it has not been previously used. When the shellac is dry, brush in a coat of stearine, making sure that all parts are coated.

Cut out pieces of burlap large enough to fit inside the pieces of the mold and trim the edges an inch or so above the edge of the mold. Cut the edge of the burlap where necessary to make it fit over any contours in the mold.

Cut a supply of burlap squares and strips in various sizes. These pieces are to be saturated with plaster and placed in the mold over the first layer of burlap. The size of the pieces needed will depend upon the size and shape of the mold you are working in. After you have made a form or two you will know in advance just about what you will need.

Mix up a bowl of molding plaster to a rather thin, creamy consistency. Dip pieces of burlap into the plaster; strip off some of the excess plaster, and lay the patch in the mold on the first layer of burlap. It is best to start in the deepest area of the mold, as this will hold the first layer of burlap down in this area. Continue to spread out from the point of beginning until you have a layer of the plastered burlap over the whole inside of the mold. Each piece should overlap the next piece a little, and at the edge it should extend beyond the edge of the mold about half an inch or so. Be sure that each piece is pressed down to fit the contour of the mold. When the first layer is finished, put in another layer in the same manner. For most forms, two layers will be enough except in certain areas. In head forms it is a good idea to put another layer in the lower jaw under the mouth so this area will be strong enough when the lip slot is cut out. In any form an extra strip or two should be put in areas where there might be stress or strain. It is always better to have the form too strong than not strong enough.

When the plaster-and-burlap lining has hardened somewhat, take a sharp knife and trim the edges even with the edge of the mold. If you do this at the right time the edges will trim smoothly and quite easily. If you try to do it too soon the edges will not cut smoothly; and if you wait too long, like overnight, the plaster will harden so much that it is hard to cut.

As soon as the edges have been trimmed, you can remove the pieces from the mold and assemble them. The pieces are fastened together by putting strips of plaster-and-burlap over the inside seam. Do not put any on the outside.

On head forms for horned or antlered animals, the antler block should be installed and held in place with pieces of burlap and plaster; and on whole animal forms the leg rods and tail wire should be installed before the form is assembled just as in the paper forms. These are also held in place with strips of burlap and plaster as shown in Fig. 46.

In assembling a whole animal form there will be seams that you are unable to reach from the inside, such as down in the legs. To bind the leg pieces together, mix a little plaster, rather thick, and put it along the edge of the form. Also, put a few wads of sisal dipped in plaster in the legs so it will contact both pieces of the form. Put the leg pieces together before this plaster sets up, and bind the leg with tape or cord to hold it firmly together until the plaster sets.

In the body part of the form you can reach most of the seams until the last piece is put in place. It will then be necessary to cut a window in the form large enough to get your arm through. You can close this opening finally by placing small strips of burlap dipped in plaster around the inside edge of the opening somewhat like a doorjamb. When this has set up, put the piece back in place with a little plaster.

Allow the manikin to dry, then give it at least one coat of shellac, and it is finished.

FIBERGLASS MANIKINS

Forms made of fiberglass are very light and strong. For ordinary jobs there is no particular advantage in using it, but in certain cases it is well worth the extra cost.

In small mammal work, whether whole mounts or head mounts, fiberglass can be very convenient. Whole or head forms can be made satisfactorily out of paper, but you will have to wait several days for them to dry. Plaster and burlap is not very practical for use in small legs or small heads because of the bulkiness of the material. In such cases, fiberglass is often the best answer.

Small head forms such as badger, fox, or bobcat can be made of fiberglass and be ready to use in an hour or so. Furthermore, you can usually turn out a better mount on them because the lips can be made thinner and more natural.

Fiberglass is also very useful in making bodies for snakes and other slender, long-bodied creatures. With fiberglass you can have strength without excess bulk or weight.

For making forms you can use ordinary polyester resin, which is a syrupy liquid which has to be mixed with a liquid catalyst immediately before using. At normal room temperature it begins to set up in twenty to thirty minutes, or even faster if a few more drops of catalyst are added.

The resin is used in conjunction with either glass cloth or glass mat material which can be purchased by the yard.

Fiberglass can be used in plaster molds, but be sure to use a good separator; otherwise, the resin will stick to the mold. There are several types of separators sold for use with fiberglass resin which work quite well. For jobs in which a lot of detail is not essential, you can use stearine if you apply it liberally. Ordinary paste floor wax also works about the same. Plastic kitchen wrap makes a positive separator, but is hard to use on some surfaces.

To make a form from fiberglass, the procedure is about the same as with other materials. Just apply the separator to the mold, put pieces of glass cloth or glass mat in the mold, and apply the resin, which you have thoroughly mixed with the catalyst. Be sure the glass cloth or mat is saturated with the resin.

The number of layers to apply depends upon the size of the form and the amount of strength required. For most forms, two layers of cloth or one layer of medium-weight glass mat will be sufficient. After you get the feel of the material, and have used it a time or two, you will know how much to use for the job at hand.

Do not mix more resin than you can use in a few minutes. When it starts to gel there is nothing you can do to stop it. If you want the resin to set up faster than normal you can use a few more drops of the catalyst than the directions call for. After you have applied the resin to the cloth, the setting time can also be speeded up by placing it in the sunshine. The heat and ultraviolet light from the sun act as an additional catalyst.

As soon as the form begins to feel dry to the touch, it may be taken from the mold, but it will continue to get harder for some time. The pieces of the form are put together by putting strips of glass cloth over the seams and applying resin.

MAKING EXCELSIOR FORMS

This method is an old one but is still used by many taxidermists. While it is inferior to the methods described above, a skilled worker can achieve remarkably good results with it, especially on long-haired animals. The skill of the operator, in fact, determines the success of any method.

This excelsior manikin is similar to the one described in Chapter 3 for small mammals, except that in this case the body is made in one unit.

In this method the leg bones and either the natural skull or an artificial one are used. All bones used must be thoroughly cleaned and treated with borax or arsenic, since they will be in the finished mount.

From your measurements and sketches of the natural body, cut out a center board for the body. This board should be the same general outline as the body but a little smaller. If the animal is to have a curve in the body, the center board may be sawed in the middle and the pieces fastened back together at an angle with pieces of strap metal.

The body is supported by iron rods which are bent to fit against the leg bones as closely as possible. The lower ends of the rods should be threaded and attached to the base with nuts and washers. The upper end is attached to the center board. If you figure the length carefully enough, the upper ends of the rods can also be threaded and attached to the center board with nuts and washers; otherwise, they can be attached with staples or U bolts. This framework is set up as shown in Fig. 31 except that the leg rods are attached through the base.

The head is also supported by rods as shown in Fig. 31. For the tail, use a double twisted wire and attach it to the center board.

When the framework is set up in the proper position, the body is built up with excelsior and string as described for making bird and small mammal bodies. In the larger animals you can partially build up the bulk of the body with wire netting or hardware cloth covered with a layer of plaster-and-burlap. This will eliminate the need for so much excelsior winding.

It is impossible to put as much muscular detail in an excelsior body as in a clay model, but in a long-haired animal this is not too important. Fig. 47 shows a bobcat form being made of excelsior.

Muscular indentations can be achieved to some extent by sewing through the excelsior with a long sacking needle and pulling the string tight.

After the body is shaped up to the best of your ability, a thin coat of papier mâché can be spread over the entire body and some additional detail modeled in.

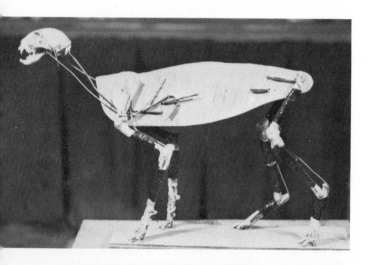

FIG. 47 An armature set up for making an excelsior bobcat form, and the resulting excelsior manikin. You can model over the manikin lightly with papier mâché to give additional muscular detail.

When the manikin is completely dry, it should be given at least two coats of shellac.

MAKING EAR LINERS

Almost all mammals except those with very small ears should have the cartilage removed from the ears before mounting. The cartilage must then be replaced with artificial ear liners at the time of mounting.

Paper or plastic ear liners can be bought for most game animals, but it is an easy matter to make your own.

When the cartilage is first removed from the ear of a fresh animal it retains its natural shape until it begins to dry. If allowed to dry it shrinks and shrivels into an almost unrecognizable object, but even a cartilage in this condition will again resume its natural shape if soaked in water for a little while. This is important to remember.

Elsewhere in this book it was recommended that in skinning game heads you turn the ears but leave the cartilage attached to the front of the ear until the skin is tanned. This is generally true, but it you wish to save the cartilages in one piece to use as a pattern for making ear liners it is better to remove them while the skin is fresh.

There may be times when you are far from home and get some animal that you will want to make ear liners for many months later. In such a case you should completely remove the cartilages while the skin is fresh. Either label the cartilages and save them or tie them to the skin. When you are finally ready to make the ear liners, all you have to do is soak the cartilages in water for a few minutes.

To make a mold, lay the cartilages in a bed of sand, back side down, and be sure that they are not bent out of shape. Mix up some plaster or hydrocal and apply it to the inside of the cartilage. Sometimes it is better to apply only a thin coat first so the weight of the plaster does not distort the ear. When you have the ear completely filled, allow the plaster to harden thoroughly, and then remove it from the ear. This will give you a perfect plaster reproduction of the inside of the ear. See Fig. 48.

To make the ear liners, cover the plaster cores with plastic kitchen wrap or aluminum foil and cut a piece of glass cloth to fit over the ear side of the covered core. The glass cloth can be held in place by winding it with a few turns of lightweight string.

FIG. 48   Plaster ear cores are made by carefully removing the cartilage from the ears and filling them with plaster. Before making fiberglass ear liners over these cores, cover them with aluminum foil or plastic kitchen wrap.

FIG. 49   Fiberglass ear liners which were made over the plaster ear cores.

Mix a little fiberglass resin with catalyst and paint it on the glass cloth, being sure that it is thoroughly saturated. When the fiberglass has hardened, trim the edges of the ear liner and remove the plaster core. This will give you a perfect fiberglass reproduction of the ear cartilage. See Fig. 49.

The plaster cores should be labeled and saved, as they can be used over and over again.

Ear liners can also be made of laminated paper. To do this the ear cores should be shellacked and coated with stearine. The paper is then pasted over the cores in layers as described for making paper manikins. The number of layers needed depends upon the size of the ear, but usually three or four layers is enough. When the paper ears are dry, they must be given several coats of shellac or lacquer to make them waterproof.

Another method that was used much in the past was to make ear liners of thin sheet lead. The lead was beaten out into the shape of the ear and trimmed to the correct shape. Around the butt of the ear, flanges were cut and beaten out to fit the contours of the head form. Small nails were driven through the skin and flanges to hold the ears securely to the head. These ear liners were usually drilled with many small holes to reduce the weight and to allow the paste to go through and hold more securely. (This is a good practice on any ear liners.)

Lead ear liners were very good in spite of their weight. They were used in some of the finest museum taxidermy that has ever been done, but plastic ear liners are now cheaper, lighter, and much easier to make.

For some animals with small, hairy ears without much detail, suitable ear liners can be made of corrugated cardboard cut to the proper shape and shellacked or lacquered. These should never be used on large-eared animals such as deer, however.

MANIKINS WITH DETACHABLE LEGS

If an animal is skinned by the seamless-leg method described in Chapter 4, it will be necessary to make a manikin with detachable legs.

The manikin may be made of laminated paper, plaster-and-burlap, or fiberglass as described above, but either during or after assembling the pieces of the manikin the legs must be cut off just below the body and a mortise joint installed in each leg. This can be done by installing two pieces of board in the upper part of the leg, with a space between, and one piece of board in the lower portion that will fit between the space. See Fig. 50. When the legs are assembled, two steel pins are inserted through all three pieces of wood to hold the leg absolutely rigid.

When manikins are made in this manner, the leg rods cannot extend all the way up the leg and into the body in the usual manner. They can only extend up as far as the point where the legs are cut off.

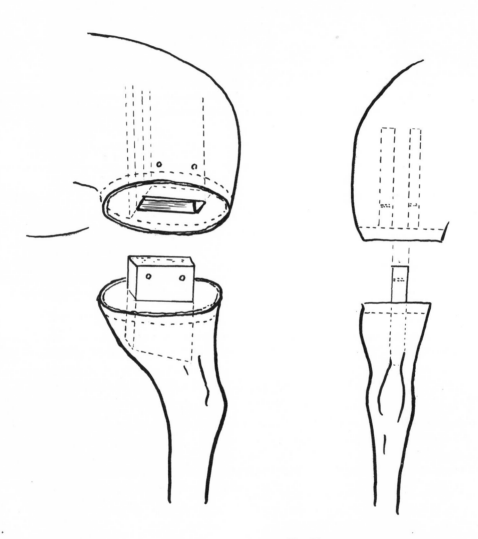

FIG. 50   If you use the seamless method of leg mounting, the legs of the manikin must be removable. Build a mortise joint into each leg as shown here.

8

Mounting Game Heads, Antlers, and Feet

The mounting of deer and other game heads is often one of the most important and lucrative parts of a taxidermist's work. The mounting of antlers, horns, and feet is also an important sideline. This is, of course, one small step in the mounting of a large mammal, but the beginner should mount at least a few heads and feet before attempting a whole large mammal. For this reason, this part of the work warrants a separate discussion.

Actually the hardest part of mounting a game head is getting everything ready to start. We will assume that you have the head form and ear liners made and the backboard for the head form cut out.

TREATMENT OF ANTLERS AND HORNS

Preparing antlers for mounting is usually not very difficult. The skull plate should, of course, be cleaned of all flesh. This can be done most easily by boiling it in water until any flesh and membrane come off easily. If the antlers have dried bloodstains or any other foreign matter on them, they should be washed with warm water and detergent. Quite often the lower, rough part of the antler is coated with resin or gummy bark from trees and bushes. This can be removed with a wire brush while you are washing the antlers.

Sometimes antlers freshly out of the velvet are too light-colored to be attractive. This is also true of old antlers which have been out in the weather or bleached by the sun for some time. To restore such antlers to a more normal color, you can stain them with a potassium permanganate solution. This is made by dissolving a teaspoonful of potassium permanganate crystals in a cup of warm water. Apply this to the antlers with a brush or cloth until the desired color is attained. This liquid is a deep purple color, but it turns brown as it dries and closely resembles the normal color of antlers. To get a natural effect, remember that antlers are not a solid color all over. They are usually darker in the low places, and the tips are usually quite light. This stain will also stain your fingers a dark-brown color if you apply it with a cloth. It is not easily washed off your hands, but it will wear off in a few days.

To give antlers a brighter, richer appearance, paint them with a mixture of 1 part linseed oil and 3 parts turpentine. Rub this off with a soft lintless cloth. It will give the antlers a soft natural luster, unlike shellac or varnish, which should never be used on antlers. If antlers are to be stained, the stain should be applied first.

Sometimes you may get a set of antlers in the velvet and wish to keep them that way. In the early stages of growth, before the antlers are near maturity, there is quite a lot of blood and moisture under the velvet, and spoilage can occur easily. These antlers should be pierced all over with a needle or sharp wire and then rubbed lightly with borax. The needle pricks will allow the moisture in the antlers to evaporate more freely. If you can keep them in a freezer for a few weeks it will dehydrate the antlers with little danger of spoilage. Antlers in the velvet should not be washed unless absolutely necessary as this is apt to spoil the appearance of the velvet.

Horns are in some cases more difficult to prepare for mounting than antlers. All animals that grow horns have a bony core that runs partway up into the horn. This core is a part of the skull, and there is usually some fleshy substance between the horn and the bony core which should be removed. The easiest way to do this is to boil several inches of the base of the horns when you are boiling the skull plate. This will usually loosen the horns enough so that they can be pulled or twisted off.

After the horns have been removed, clean off any fleshy substance from the inside and from the core. Sometimes the core and the base of the horns are very greasy and should be washed in gasoline. Before putting the horns back on the core, it is a good practice to paint the core and inside of the horns with formaldehyde and then dust them with borax or arsenic. You can put a little water putty or modeling composition, Formula #6, inside the horns before replacing them. A small finishing nail or two should also be driven through the back base of the horn into the bony core to eliminate danger of the horn being pulled off again.

Horns that are dirty may be washed with water and detergent; but such horns as sheep and antelope should never have any oily substance applied to them as was recommended for antlers.

When the horns or antlers are ready, they are attached to the head form by putting three or four screws through the skull plate into the antler block in the head form. See Fig. 51. The skull plate should then be modeled over as shown in Fig. 52.

To prepare the tanned head skin, or cape, for mounting, it must either be soaked in warm borax water or be thoroughly sponged on the flesh side until it is completely wet and relaxed. Skins with soft, wooly hair such as that of the mountain goat should be sponged, but skins such as that of the deer can be soaked.

If the cartilage is still attached to the front of the ears, they may require a little additional soaking, as the cartilage will take longer to relax than the rest of the skin.

When the ear cartilages are pliable, carefully separate them from the skin. After they have been through the tanning process it is usually not easy to remove the cartilage in one piece. You may have to peel or cut it off in pieces. A little narrow shaving beam as shown in Fig. 26 is handy for working on the ears.

Hang the skin up and squeeze out the excess water; then you are ready to start the actual mounting.

Insert the ear liners and check to see if they fit properly. If the front of the ear skin will not fit against the liner without strain, you should trim a little off the edges of the liner.

Put a little skin paste, Formula #1, in the ears and spread it around so the whole inside of the ear skin is coated. Spread some

FIG. 51 Antlers are generally fastened to the head with screws. Be sure the screws are long enough to go well into the antler block in the head form.

FIG. 52 After the antlers are attached, model over the skull plate with papier mâché.

more paste on the ear liners and insert them in the ears. Press the ears all over with your fingers and see that the skin makes contact with the liners at all points. If you have a clipper-type stapler it is a good idea to staple through the ears in several places.

If you have not already cut a mouth slot in the head form, this should be done before you go any further. See Fig. 53. This can be done most easily with a saber saw, but you can do it with a small coping saw by boring a starting hole. Do not make the slot too

FIG. 53 A deer head form with the mouth slot cut out to receive the lip skin.

wide, but it should be wide enough to get both the upper and lower lip skin through by using a little force.

To proceed, spread some skin paste on the head and front part of the neck of the head form. Also, spread some paste on the inside of the head skin and down the middle of the neck.

Put the skin on the form and arrange it in place so the eyeholes are over the eyesockets in the form. Pull the skin up so it fits snugly around the horns or antlers, and put a small nail on each side somewhere to hold the skin more or less in place. See that the skin is not twisted to one side down the front of the neck. If it is a shoulder mount, be sure the brisket is in the proper place on the form. Now, turn the head over with the back of the neck up, and start sewing up the incision. Use a three-cornered hide needle or a curved surgical needle and strong waxed thread. All stitches should be made from the inside of the skin so you will not pull hair through the skin with the thread. Start sewing at one antler and sew to the bottom of the V formed by the incision. Tie the thread securely there, then start at the other antler and sew all the way down the neck.

If the skin does not come together easily along the seam, it usually will if you slide the skin forward a little on the form. Sometimes it is necessary to use pliers or skin pullers and quite a bit of force to pull the skin together.

When you get to the end of the form, sew an inch or so farther and tie the thread securely. Any excess skin should be cut off about 2 inches back of the form. This extra skin is folded over inside the form, and then the backboard is put in place. Small rust-resistant nails are driven through the skin and form into the edge of the backboard.

If you have not yet put a hanger on the backboard you should do so now so that the head can be hung on the wall. If the head of the mount is turned much to either side, it may be necessary to place the hanger a little off center to make the head hang straight.

With the head hanging up, adjust the skin on the face. Back off and look at it from a distance to make sure it is symmetrical. Apply more paste to the head through the mouth area, and with a screwdriver or some other flat tool, force the upper and lower lip skin through the mouth slot.

If necessary, put a little modeling compound in the nose area and arrange the nostrils in the correct shape. You can put a little wad of paper in each nostril to hold the skin in place until the paste sets up.

Put some modeling compound in the eyesockets and under the eyelids, if needed, and set the glass eyes. If you have taken the measurement between the eyeballs as recommended in Chapter 4, you can use this measurement now; otherwise, just use your best judgment of how deep to set the eyes. If your animal has elliptical pupils, such as the deer, be sure that the pupils are pointing in the right direction.

You should now give your attention to the ears. Mix some modeling compound very thick, so it is not sticky, and put pieces of this down inside the ears to form the ear butts. When you have enough of the compound in place, model the ear butts into the proper shape through the skin, and arrange the ears in the desired poisition. It may be necessary to tie or otherwise hold the ears in position until the composition sets up. When the ears are properly arranged, you can put a wad of paper or cloth in each ear to hold the skin firmly against the ear liners until it is dry.

Feel over the whole mount and see that there are no air bubbles under the skin. If there are, punch them a few times with an icepick or awl and force the air out. Drive some pins in all the muscular depressions to hold the skin down in these areas until the paste sets up. These pins will be pulled out later, so do not drive them all the way in.

Wash off any paste that might have gotten on the hair, and let the specimen dry.

FINISHING THE HEAD

When the mount is completely dry, some finishing will be necessary around the eyes, nose, and probably the ears. If the eyelids have shrunk slightly away from the glass eyes, this crack should be filled in with black wax. See Formula #4 in the Appendix.

The nose should be stained or painted the correct color and the nostrils smoothed inside, if necessary, with modeling composition or pink acrylic plastic and then stained the correct color.

An airbrush is excellent for applying color to the eyelids and nose, but a small brush can be used instead.

If the ears need any additional filling, this can be done with modeling composition which is then stained.

OTHER GAME HEADS

Game head mounts other than those with antlers or horns are done in exactly the same manner except that you have no horns to contend with.

If such heads as those of bear or cats are to be mounted with the mouth open, the artificial teeth may be set in the form before mounting. However, if the skin has good inside lip skin, it is better to mount the head first and paste the lip skin down inside the mouth where it belongs. The artificial jaws can then be set against the lip skin and fastened in place before the backboard is installed in the form.

MOUNTING ANTLERS ON A PANEL

Many sportsmen wish to have horns or antlers mounted on a wall panel without having the whole head mounted. This is usually not very difficult, but is sometimes more of a problem than you would expect.

The skull plate should, of course, be cleaned and treated as if it were to be mounted on a head.

If you place the sawed portion of the skull plate against the wall, the antlers will stick out in an unnatural and unattractive position. The skull plate will, therefore, need to be cut again so that the antlers will stand up in a more natural position. See Fig. 54.

Usually, on an antler mount, the skull plate is modeled over with papier mâché or some other modeling composition and finally covered with leather, velvet, or some other material.

If this is to be done, do not attach the skull plate directly to the wall panel. Instead, cut a more or less circular piece of wood a little

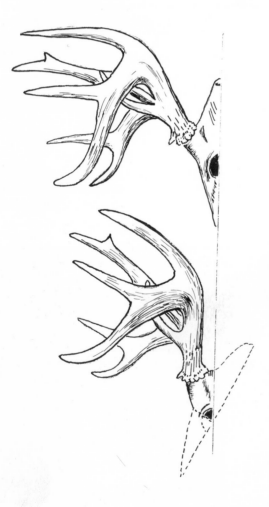

FIG. 54   When mounting antlers on a wall panel, cut the skull plate at an angle that will make the antlers hang in an attractive position. The top sketch shows the skull plate cut as if for a head form; this makes the antlers seem to droop. The bottom sketch shows a proper cut for a wall panel.

larger than the skull plate. Attach this to the wall panel and then attach the skull plate to this block. See Fig. 55. This will give you something to attach the leather or other material to after you model over the skull plate and block.

There are many attractive ways that an antler mount can be finished. Fig. 56 shows a mount that is covered with buckskin and decorated with strips of buckskin that were cut with a pinking machine.

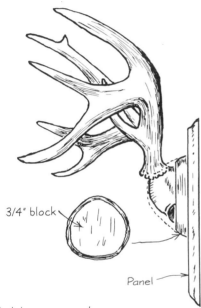

FIG. 55   Attach a more-or-less circular block of the proper size to the panel first, and then attach the antlers to this block. This will give you something to attach the leather or cloth covering to.

3/4" block

Panel

Model over area shown by dotted line – then cover with leather or other material.

FIG. 56   A finished antler mount, with skull plate modeled over and covered with buckskin.

MOUNTING CATTLE HORNS

Sometimes a taxidermist is called upon to mount cattle horns that may or may not have been removed from the skull. Such horns are usually to be polished also. When mounting these horns it is usually better not to use the skull plate and bony core, as this only adds to the weight of the finished mount.

These horns are best mounted by making a straight wooden core which fits into the ends of the horns. The distance between the horns should be about the same as it would be on the skull. The horns are held to the core by means of small nails or screws which are put through the horn into the core near the inside edge of the horns. The exposed part of the wood core is modeled over and covered with leather or some other material. This covering should cover the ends of the horns enough to hide the nails or screws which hold the horn to the core.

If the horns are to be polished, this should be done before they are mounted. To do a good job of polishing, the horns must be made absolutely smooth. The easiest way to smooth down rough spots is to scrape them with the broken edge of a piece of glass and then finish with fine sandpaper.

After all roughness has been removed, the horns may be polished with a mixture of linseed oil and powdered pumice stone. Make a thin paste of this mixture and apply it to the horns with a cloth. The more you rub, the brighter the polish. Finish the polishing with a soft dry cloth. If you have a buffing wheel to fit on a motor or on an electric drill it will save a lot of labor.

MOUNTING FEET

The feet of deer, elk, and other animals can be used to make attractive gun racks, lamp bases, and other items. You can buy ready-made forms for mounting feet, but it is an easy matter to make your own.

When you skin out the leg of a deer or other animal, disjoint the leg at the last joint, which is down in the base of the hoof. Leave the tendons attached to the leg bone. Bend the leg bone to the shape wanted, such as for a gun rack or a lamp base, and keep it in that position until it is dry and stiff. When it is dry, model over it slightly with a little clay to make it nice and smooth; then make a mold of it in two parts. See Fig. 57. When the mold is dry, shellac it and grease the inside with stearine. The upper part of the bone should be cut off at the right length before making the mold.

To make forms from the mold, bend a piece of threaded rod to fit inside the mold, letting the upper end stick out as much as will be needed. Fill the mold with plaster or hydrocal. When this hardens, take it out and you will have a reproduction of the leg to mount the skin over.

Many taxidermists do not bother to mount the legs when making gun racks. Instead, they just bend the unskinned leg into the position wanted and let it dry thoroughly. The legs are then sawed off to the desired length and a threaded rod is driven into the hole in the leg bone.

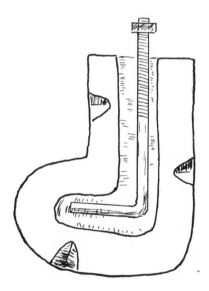 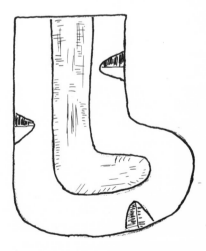

FIG. 57   Two halves of mold for a gun-rack foot mount. Notice notches and keys in edges of mold to ensure proper alignment. A threaded rod or bolt is placed in the mold before it is filled.

If this method is used, the marrow should be cleaned out of the bone as thoroughly as possible and the hole washed out with gasoline to remove the oil in the bone as much as possible. You can then put some epoxy glue in the leg bone before inserting the rod and it will usually hold quite well.

Legs treated in this manner are, of course, subject to attacks by insects, but they usually keep amazingly well.

If the hoofs of mounted feet are to be polished, this can be done in the same way as described for cattle horns.

9

Mounting Large Mammals

In this chapter we will be concerned mainly with the correct procedure for mounting the skin on the manikin. It is assumed that you have the manikin finished as described in Chapter 7, and that the mouth slot has been cut out and the ear liners made.

Although a large animal can be mounted by one person, the task is much easier if you have someone to assist you in at least part of the operation.

Perhaps it should be mentioned here that if the animal is one with horns or antlers, these should not be attached to the manikin in advance, as you will not be able to get the skin on over them.

If the animal is one with rather short hair on the hocks, such as the deer, a mold should be made of the hock area on each side of both hind legs of the manikin. See Fig. 58.

A small piece of rope or heavy cord of the proper size is glued to the manikin to represent the prominent leg vein which runs down over the hock area of most animals. The mold is then made over this. If the rope vein is pulled off the leg with the mold, be sure to glue it back in the same place.

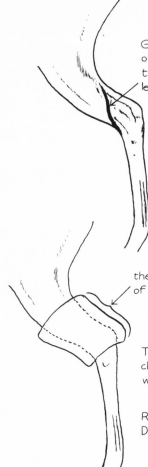

Glue piece of cord
or soft rope to manikin
to represent this prominent
leg vein

then make mold of each side
of leg over this area

These molds will be temporarily
clamped back on over skin
when animal is mounted.

Results: Beautiful
Detail of Hock Area

FIG. 58 Procedure for making a mold of the hock area of a manikin. The time and effort required pays off when you're mounting a short-haired animal such as a deer.

These hock molds will be used later. They are not absolutely necessary, but they will enable you to greatly enhance the appearance of your mount, and are well worth the extra trouble it takes to make them.

The skin should be soaked in warm borax water until it is thoroughly relaxed. Hang it up to drain and squeeze out as much excess water as possible. Do any additional trimming that may be needed around the eyes, lips, and nose. Check the ear liners, and when they fit properly they may be pasted in the ears.

If the tail wires have not been wrapped, this should also be done now. Cut the wires off to the proper length and build the tail up to the proper size by winding with sisal and string.

You can apply some skin paste, Formula #1, to the head, neck, and back area of the manikin before putting the skin on, but it is usually less messy to put the skin over the manikin first and then lift it where necessary to apply the paste under it.

Lift the skin over the manikin and arrange it approximately in place. Fold the body skin back toward the head and apply paste to the back area and partway down the sides. Straighten the skin back out again and slide it into position along the back. Fit the tail skin on the tail and sew up the tail. This will hold the skin in place at the rear end of the body.

If the horns or antlers have not been attached, this can be done now. When the antlers are securely fastened, model over the skull plate with modeling composition, Formula#6, and while this is setting up you can go ahead and work on the rest of the body.

A little modeling composition may be needed in the feet. Start with one foot and with strong waxed thread and a three-cornered hide needle, sew up the leg to a point just below the knee or hock after applying paste to that portion of the leg. Take small stitches and insert the needle from the inside on each stitch. Next, sew up the same leg on the other side about the same distance. Keep the work as clean as possible, and wash off any paste that gets on the hair before it has a chance to dry.

By the time all four legs have been sewed up a short distance, the modeling on the skull plate should be hard, and you can work on that area again.

Apply paste to the head and neck areas, being sure to get it in all the depressions in the neck. Start sewing at one antler and sew up the head and neck as described in the preceding chapter. Also, finish mounting the head in the same manner.

At this time it is usually easier if you turn the animal over on its back. When this is done, apply paste to the upper legs, one at a time, and sew them up almost to the body. Pull the belly skin together and see if it is going to fit properly. If it does not come together easily, use pliers or skin pullers and pull the edges until it does fit.

Sometimes there is quite a bit of excess skin at the union of the legs and body underneath. If this is the case, you can cut a narrow slot in the manikin between the leg and body and stuff the excess skin into this slot.

When you have finished sewing the legs and belly, turn the animal back over on its feet and inspect the body. If there are air bubbles under the skin in places, punch these areas with an icepick or awl and force the air out. If there seems to be excess skin in places it does not necessarily mean that the body is not the right size. The excess skin can usually be taken up by making a series of small wrinkles in the skin instead of one large wrinkle.

Drive pins partway in to hold the skin down in all the depressions or concave surfaces of the body until the paste sets up.

If you made molds of the hocks as described earlier, sand or rasp the inside of these molds down a little to partially compensate for the thickness of the skin and put the molds back on the hocks. They can be held in place with C-clamps. The molds should be taken off in about an hour to see if the skin under them is seated properly. Make any correction necessary and put the molds back on for a day or so.

Before leaving the specimen to dry, be sure that all paste is washed off the hair. It is hard to remove if it is allowed to dry. The day after mounting, the specimen should be inspected again. At this time you can pull the pins out and comb and brush the hair. After the animal is thoroughly dry, the head should be finished as described in the preceding chapter.

MOUNTING BY THE SEAMLESS-LEG METHOD

If the animal was skinned by the seamless-leg method described in Chapter 4, and your manikin was made with detachable legs as described in Chapter 7, the procedure is as follows:

Place the skin over the manikin and fit it along the back. Remove one leg from the manikin, coat it with the skin paste, and also put some paste inside the leg skin. Work the leg down into the skin and slide the skin around until it fits properly. Put the leg back on the manikin and insert the steel pins to hold it in place. Repeat this on the opposite leg and then on the other two legs. You can then proceed with sewing up the belly and back of the neck as previously described. This method is quite a bit more work and trouble than the usual method of splitting the legs all the way, but it produces a beautiful result since no seams are visible in the finished mount.

MOUNTING AN ELEPHANT, RHINOCEROS, OR HIPPOPOTAMUS

While it is very unlikely that you will ever be called upon to mount an elephant, a brief description of the process might be of interest since it is quite different from the process for mounting other mammals.

The fresh skin of an elephant may weigh as much as 2,500 pounds and is up to 2½ inches thick in places. This skin must be shaved down to a quarter-inch or less in thickness and then tanned as in the case of other animals. Since a skin of such weight and proportions cannot be handled in one piece, it is generally cut in four to six pieces at the time of skinning.

There have been several methods employed in the mounting of such beasts, but basically the procedure is to build a strong framework, or armature, which is covered with wire netting and plaster. This framework should be about 3 inches smaller in all dimensions than the natural body. This structure is then covered with modeling clay and modeled roughly into shape. The tanned and relaxed skin is put over the clay model and worked into shape from the outside. More clay is pumped under the skin if needed.

When the skin is completely modeled into shape, the outside of the skin is given a thin clay wash and a plaster mold is made over the skin in sections. The clay wash will allow the plaster to stick to the skin, but acts as a partial separator so it can be removed later.

The plaster mold with the skin attached is removed from the clay model and the skin is cleaned inside. About two layers of plaster and burlap are then applied to the inside of the skin, leaving the skin sandwiched between two layers of plaster, where it remains until it is dry. The plaster and burlap is then removed from the inside. The original method was to then coat the inside of the skin with three layers of papier mâché reinforced with screen wire. Each layer was allowed to dry and was shellacked before applying the next layer. After that it was further reinforced with wooden ribs which were cut to conform to the contours of the surface. Nowadays this elaborate reinforcement system could be eliminated by the use of fiberglass.

After the sections are all so treated, they are removed from the plaster mold and assembled except for the head. You then have to get inside the body through the neck opening and fasten the various sections together from the inside. The two halves of the head are then put together and attached to the rest of the body from the outside. The seams between the different sections of the body are filled and touched up to match the skin.

PORPOISES AND WHALES

Aquatic mammals such as the porpoise and whale are usually handled in the same manner as sharks, which are discussed in Chapter 12. The physical structure and texture of the skin on these creatures makes it impractical to mount them by conventional methods. Much more satisfactory results can be attained by making a complete mold of the specimen and making a cast either in fiberglass or plaster-and-burlap. The cast may then be colored in the same manner as a mounted fish.

Fig. 59 shows a fiberglass reproduction of a freshwater porpoise from the Amazon River in South America. The natural teeth were used in this cast, but the rest of the body is fiberglass and weighs less than 10 pounds.

FIG. 59   A fiberglass replica of a freshwater porpoise from the Amazon River. It was made from a plaster mold taken of one of several specimens captured by Ross Allen in 1955 and flown back to the United States alive.

10

Making Fur Rugs

In some localities the making of fur rugs is the most important part of the commercial taxidermist's work. Many people do not care to own mounted game heads, fish, or other trophies, but there is always a good market for well-made fur rugs.

All methods ordinarily used in the making or rugs are somewhat similar, although several techniques are employed.

After many year's experience in this type of work, I have found the following procedure to be most satisfactory.

Soak the head and neck portion of the tanned skin in warm borax water until it is thoroughly soft and relaxed.

Squeeze out the excess water and do any trimming that is necessary about the head. See that the lips are properly split and shaved thin. Give special attention to the nose, and cut away all cartilage from this area. If the cartilage was not removed from the ears before tanning, peel it away now.

At this stage you should have the ear liners made, but if not, you can make them quickly from corrugated cardboard as described in Chapter 7.

Coat the ear liners with skin paste, Formula #1, and insert them in the ears. Place a ball of modeling composition, Formula #6, in the base of each ear. Coat the head form with skin paste, put the skin over the form, and work it into place. See that the eyeholes are level and in the right position. Lift the upper lip and put as much modeling composition in the nose area as is needed. Model the nose into the proper shape and stuff a small wad of paper into each nostril to hold them open. Put more paste on the lip skin and fold the lips over inside the mouth of the form.

Drive pins or small nails in all depressions to hold the skin down in these areas until the paste sets up. These pins are to be pulled out later, so do not drive them in all the way.

Put some modeling composition in the eyes and set the glass eyes. Shape the skin carefully around the eyes and use pins where necessary to hold it in place.

The skin around the lower edge of the head form should be tacked or stapled to the form to prevent shrinkage while drying.

When the head is dry, or almost so, the artificial jaws may be set in the form. Put them in place against the lip skin, which was folded over inside the head form. The jaws are held in place with modeling composition or with strips of burlap dipped in plaster. Fig. 60 shows a rug head before the artificial jaws were installed, and Fig. 61 shows the finished head.

After the jaws are securely set, you can do any modeling that is necessary inside the mouth. The cheeks always need to be modeled in on each side of the jaws, and a little modeling is also needed around the edge of the jaws. When this modeling is completely dry it can be finished with paint or you can apply a layer of the pink acrylic plastic which is recommended in Chapter 11 for making artificial jaws. When this plastic is used in the cheek area it actually bonds the upper and lower jaws together and makes a single unit of the whole mouth. It closely resembles the actual skin color and texture of the inside of the mouth. It can be stained darker in areas where needed by using very thin paint.

The nose, lips, and eyelids should be stained or painted the correct color. An airbrush is best for this, but it can be done with a small artist's brush. A final coat of shellac or clear gloss lacquer will give these parts a wet look, but do not use lacquer unless you used lacquer to paint the areas in the first place.

For the rest of the work you will need a table large enough to

FIG. 60 A black bear rug head, ready for installation of the artificial teeth and tongue.

FIG. 61 The same head, completed.

accommodate the stretched-out skin. Perhaps it should be said here that you do not have to finish the head completely before you proceed with the rest of the work. As soon as you mount the head you can go ahead and do the preliminary work that needs to be done on the body part of the skin. The modeling and finishing work on the head can be done last if you prefer.

Turn the skin over on the table, fur side down. You should either put some padding under the head so it will not rest on the ears or let the ears hang over the edge of the table as shown in Fig. 62. Have the head centered at the edge of the table, and put a nail through the center of the back portion of the head form to hold it there.

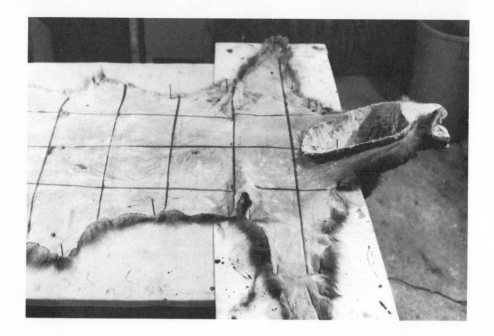

FIG. 62   Blocking a bear skin in preparation for making a rug. If the mounted head is allowed to hang over the edge of the table, it will be easier to stretch out the body skin.

Spread the skin out in all directions, and put a nail through the base of the tail into the centerline of the table.

Sponge warm borax water over the entire flesh side of the skin, and let it lie for a few minutes until it is more or less relaxed. You do not have to get the skin soppy wet, just fairly damp. The skin will relax faster if the water is quite warm. Sometimes it is necessary to dip the feet in the water for a few seconds to relax them enough to spread out properly.

When the skin is relaxed, stretch it out and make it lie as flat as possible. Pull both the front and hind legs in the direction that causes the fewest wrinkles in the skin. Put a nail through each foot to hold it in place. You will not be able to get rid of all the wrinkles. It is always necessary to cut wedges in a few places to remove the wrinkles and make the skin lie perfectly flat. See Fig. 63.

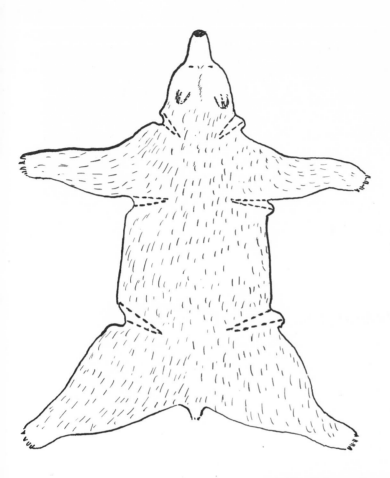

FIG. 63   It is usually necessary to cut several wedges out of the skin to make a rug lie perfectly flat. Do this after the skin has been stretched out on the work table and dampened.

Be very careful in cutting out the wedges that you do not cut out too much and create more wrinkles. The best way is to make a cut on one side of the wrinkle from the edge of the skin to the end of the wrinkle. Let one cut edge overlap the other, then draw a line on the lower flap, using the cut edge as a guide. You can then tell exactly how much to cut out.

The skin should be tacked down every few inches all around the outside edge. When all necessary wedges have been cut out and the skin lies flat, it must be trimmed to make it symmetrical. Do not trust your eyesight alone for this. The surest way is to mark parallel lines on the skin in each direction, starting with a centerline down the middle. See Fig. 64. After doing this you can measure from the corresponding line on each side to the edge of the skin and trim the

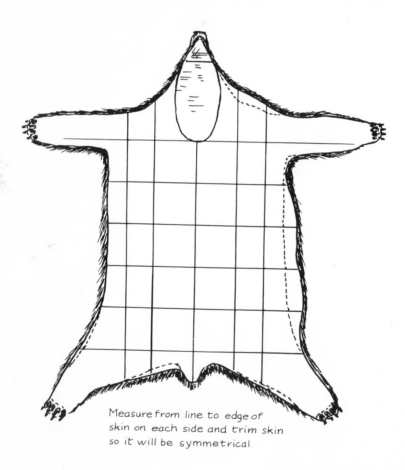

Measure from line to edge of skin on each side and trim skin so it will be symmetrical.

FIG. 64   The easiest way to make a rug skin symmetrical is to draw parallel lines on the hide, then measure from corresponding lines on each side and trim as necessary.

larger side to match the other. After this is done, sew up the cuts where the wedges were removed, using stitches as shown in Fig. 65.

Some skins are very sparsely haired in the flank area and under the front legs. Sometimes you can manage to cut out at least part of these areas in cutting out the wedges, but sometimes you cannot. If these more or less bare areas remain, they should be dyed with a

FIG. 65 When sewing the skin back together where you have cut out wedges, use a stitch like this so that the stitches will not be visible from the hair side.

good penetrating leather dye. The dye is best applied from the flesh side of the skin until it penetrates and colors the hair side. Use black or brown dye, whichever is nearest the color of the hair. Sparsely haired areas treated in this way are not nearly as unsightly as if left natural. Most rugs look better if the entire edge of the skin is also dyed.

If you do much rug work you will eventually accumulate a lot of scraps of skins. It is well to save the best of these, as they can often be used for patching bad areas in other rugs.

Leave the skin tacked down until it is dry; then turn it over and you are ready to sew on the felt borders. Ordinarily, two felt borders with pinked edges are used. The upper border, the one next to the skin, should be visible all the way around the skin, and the under border should extend out about half an inch beyond the upper border.

Most taxidermy supply houses sell 3-inch-wide strips of felt with one edge pinked. These are handy if you make only an occasional rug, but if you do much rug work a pinking machine is a good investment. They can be bought for about thirty dollars and will not only save you money, they will enable you to do a much neater job.

If you use the felt strips, the two borders can be sewn together with the correct overlap and then sewn to the skin. It is usually helpful to staple the felt to the skin with a clipper-type stapler to hold it in place while it is being sewn. The felt can be sewn to the skin with a sewing machine except around the feet and head, but hand sewing is better and just about as fast.

The biggest disadvantage in using precut felt strips is that the inside edge of the felt must be folded and puckered to make it fit around the outside curves of the skin, and the outside edge puckered to fit around the inside curves. Also, in order to look neat, the felt needs to be wider in some places than in others, especially if the skin has rather long hair.

If you have a pinking machine, a much neater job can be done by buying your felt by the yard and cutting it yourself to fit the section of the skin you are going to put it on. To do this, slip the felt under the section of skin you are going to put it on and cut the felt around this area as wide as you want the border to be. See Fig. 66. Remove this piece, pink the outside edge, then put it back and staple it to the skin. Continue to do this all the way around the skin. Do the inside, or top, border first and then the outside, or bottom, border, in the same manner. By doing this you can have the same amount of felt showing all the way around the rug and both borders will be flat.

After both borders have been stapled in place, they should be sewn securely to the skin either by machine or by hand. If you sew by hand, use a curved needle and make the stitches as shown in Fig. 67. A good strong thread such as button and carpet thread is excellent for this.

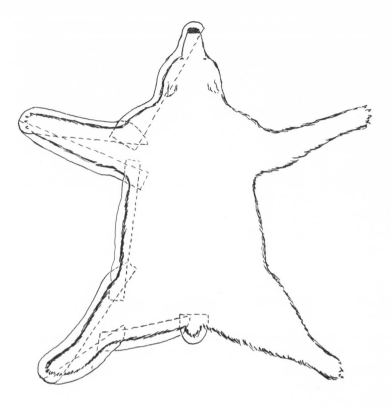

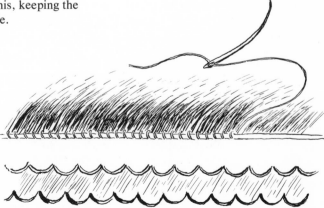

FIG. 66   When putting felt on a rug, instead of running a solid piece of felt under the entire skin, cut it to fit under one edge at a time. You will not waste as much felt and the appearance of the rug will be improved.

FIG. 67   When sewing the felt borders to the skin, use a stitch like this, keeping the stitches as even as possible.

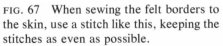

If you wish to use padding on the rug, this should be put on next. The padding goes between the skin and the bottom lining, which will go on later. Padding is not always used, but it makes a softer, more luxurious rug. Blanket, or some similar material, makes a good padding, or you can use sheet foam rubber in any thickness you want. This should be cut to fit just inside the stitches which hold the felt to the skin, and then put under the inside flaps of felt and sewn to them. On large rugs the padding should also be stitched to the skin in a few places to hold it more securely.

The underlining should be a good-quality, strong material that does not show soil too easily. Spread the material out on the table, face side down. Lay the rug on the material and cut it out even with the outside felt border. Pin the felt and lining together in several places and turn the rug back over with the lining up.

Fold the edge of the lining under about an inch all the way around the rug, leaving about an inch of felt showing. On the inside curves it will be necessary to cut the lining in places so it will fold under evenly. See Fig. 68. Pin the folded lining to the felt every few inches to hold it in place. When the entire edge has been folded under and pinned, it is sewn to the felt. Fig. 69 shows a fast, neat stitch for sewing on the lining.

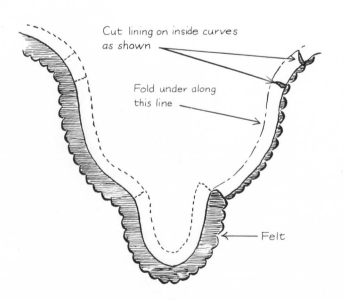

Cut lining on inside curves as shown

Fold under along this line

Felt

FIG. 68   Before you sew the bottom lining on a rug, turn the edge of the cloth neatly under. You will have to make some cuts in the edge of the cloth along inside curves.

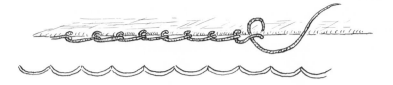

FIG. 69   A fast, neat stitch for sewing the bottom lining to the felt.

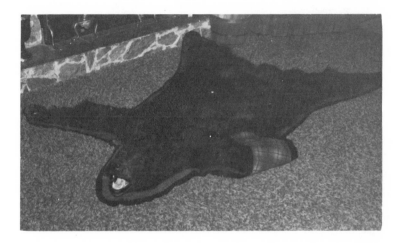

FIG. 70   A finished bearskin rug, showing the plaid lining.

Many taxidermists let the bottom layer of felt extend all the way under the rug and do not use a cloth bottom lining. This, however, leaves a rather irregular row of stitches plainly visible on the bottom of the felt which looks rather unsightly and unprofessional.

Some skins which are not suitable for a head mount rug will make a beautiful flat rug. Many people, in fact, prefer these to a rug with a mounted head. Scraps of skin which are often thrown away can also be used sometimes to make a flat rug. Fig. 71 shows a flat rug made from a white calfskin, and Fig. 72 shows a top and bottom view of an unfinished rug being made from scraps of bear skin.

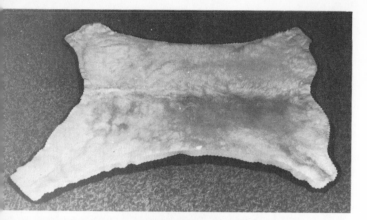

FIG. 71 A very attractive rug made from a white calfskin. Cattle skins can be bought very cheaply and made into salable items.

FIG. 72 A patch rug made from scraps of bearskin, and a bottom view of the same rug, not yet lined, showing how the pieces are sewn together.

11

Making Artificial Teeth, Tongues, and Eyes

For many years the only teeth used in open-mouth mounts were the natural teeth of the animal. Nothing could have been more natural, but after a few years the natural teeth become quite brittle and begin to crack and break very easily. Needless to say, a snaggletooth mount is unsightly.

The next advance was to use teeth carved out of ivory or cast in celluloid. This was an improvement in some ways, but it was a time-consuming and painstaking operation to make them.

With the development of plastics, quick advances were made which proved a boon to taxidermists as well as dentists. Taxidermy supply houses now sell complete plastic jaws equipped with plastic or rubber tongues. These are available for most of the animals that one is likely to get for mounting. They are a great time-saver and are far superior to anything that was used in the past. The commercially made teeth are made by an injection-mold process in which a melted plastic is injected into a mold and hardened. The plastic closely resembles the color of most natural teeth, but the gums and roof of the mouth are painted pink and look rather painted. If you

use only a few sets of artificial teeth each year, these are well worth
the money; but if you do a fairly large volume of open-mouth work
you can save several dollars on each job by making your own
without sacrificing quality. You can, in fact, make artificial teeth
and tongues that look more natural than most of the commercially
made ones, and for a fraction of the cost. After your molds are
made it takes only a few minutes to make the teeth whenever you
need them. This eliminates the necessity of keeping money tied up
in a supply of artificial teeth, or waiting for an order to arrive before
finishing a job.

The procedure is quite simple. The only materials needed to start
with are a little modeling clay, a can of dental impression material,
and some acrylic plastic resin and catalyst. The impression material and acrylic plastics can be bought from any dental supply
company.

Dental impression material is made in several forms, but the best
kind to use in this case is the powder form. The acrylic plastic also
comes in powder form and requires a liquid catalyst to make it set
up. There are two types of acrylic. One is a cold-cure type which
sets up at room temperature in a few minutes, and the other is a
heat-curing type which has to be put in boiling water to make it set
up. The cold-cure type is the easiest to use and is most satisfactory
for this work. Both types come in pink and in various light shades
which can be used for the teeth. One shade called "incisal" is quite
good for most animal teeth.

The procedure is as follows:

Remove the lower jaw from a freshly skinned head. Place both
the upper and lower jaws on the workbench with the teeth pointing
upward. Build a clay wall around the gum line just below the base
of the teeth as shown in Fig. 73.

Mix some of the dental impression material with water according
to the directions on the can. (For this work it is usually better to
use a little more water than recommended.) Stir the mixture
quickly and spoon it over the teeth and jaws.

When the material has jelled, which will be almost immediately,
you can make a plaster cap or mother mold over it if needed. If the
impression material is put on quite thick, however, this will not be
necessary.

After the impression is ready, it may be pulled off the teeth and
used immediately. Because of the high water content of this mate-

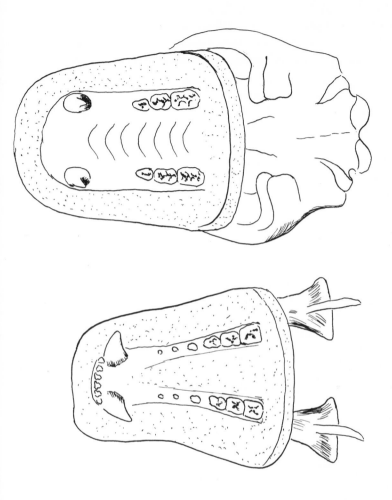

FIG. 73   A skull with the lower jaw
removed. A clay wall is built around the
jaws in preparation for making an
impression.

rial it shrinks quite fast, but it will retain its shape for several hours,
or longer, which will give you time to make many sets of teeth.

The acrylic plastic is usually sold in a dispenser bottle similar to
a mustard or catsup dispenser. The liquid catalyst may be dis-
pensed with a medicine dropper if a dispenser bottle is not fur-
nished with it.

Put a few drops of the catalyst in the tooth prints in the impression; then add enough of the tooth-colored powder to absorb the liquid. Keep adding more liquid and more powder until the tooth prints are full right up to the gum line.

When the tooth imprints have all been filled, change to the pink powder and cover the gum and mouth areas. Keep adding more liquid to the powder as you go. When the pink plastic has been built up enough so that it is no longer transparent, it will probably be thick enough. If you are using the cold-cure plastic it will set up at room temperature in a few minutes, but if you want to speed it up you can dip or place the filled impression in a pail of hot tap water for a minute or two and the plastic will set up immediately.

To make a permanent-type mold, use a good set of plastic teeth you have made from the impression-material mold and made a rubber mold over them as described in Chapter 6. Since it takes several days to make a rubber mold, it is not advisable to try to make it over a fresh skull. A good rubber mold will last for many months.

When making a rubber mold it is best to make a plaster mother mold over it. The rubber is quite flexible and the plaster cap will prevent any distortion. Fig. 74 shows some rubber molds and plastic teeth.

MAKING PLASTIC TONGUES

Tongues can also be made of the pink acrylic by making an impression or mold of the natural tongue, or a model of it. It is much easier to make a mold of a model then of the real tongue. It is good to make a plaster cast first, then make a rubber mold over it. You can keep the plaster tongues and make a new rubber mold over it whenever the old mold begins to wear out. Fig. 75 shows some plaster tongues, one of which has a rubber mold over it.

If you are mounting an animal with the mouth open very slightly, and are using a hard plastic tongue, it will be necessary to attach the tongue to the lower jaw before the teeth are installed in the head form; otherwise, you might not be able to get the tongue into the mouth. If the mouth is open wider it is best to wait until later to install the tongue as this will give you more room to do any finishing work inside the mouth.

FIG. 74   Plastic teeth and tongues being made from rubber molds.

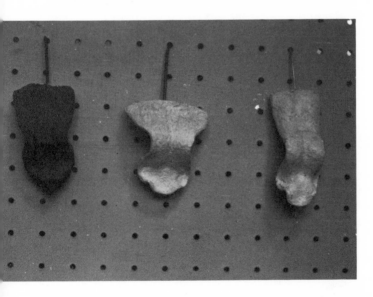

FIG. 75   Tongues can be made of plaster and kept as models. A new rubber mold can be made over them whenever needed. The tongue on the left has a rubber mold on it.

To install a plastic tongue, all you have to do is put a little acrylic powder on the lower jaw just behind the front teeth, wet it with the catalyst, and put the tongue in place.

MAKING ARTIFICIAL EYES

Before World War II, almost all glass eyes were made in Europe and were of superb quality. Furthermore, they were obtainable at reasonable prices. During the war, and in the years following, these eyes became harder and harder to get, and the prices went up accordingly. American manufacturers then started producing eyes. At first the quality was inferior to the European-made eyes, but it has now improved considerably. Like everything else, though, the price of these eyes has increased so much that a busy commercial taxidermy studio must spend hundreds of dollars each year on eyes alone. For this reason, or just for your own satisfaction, you might want to consider making at least some of your eyes yourself.

The initial cost of getting set up to produce glass eyes would be prohibitive to most people, but you can produce plastic eyes in your shop that are almost impossible to distinguish from the commercially made glass eyes after they are set in the specimen. Furthermore, the cost of producing them is almost negligible. The only disadvantage is that plastic is not as hard as glass, and plastic eyes will scratch more easily than glass eyes. After a specimen is mounted, however, there is usually not much danger of the eyes being scratched anyway. Even if they do get scratched it can easily be remedied by spraying with a clear plastic spray.

Ordinary polyester or epoxy resin is not clear enough for making eyes, but you can get clear casting resin which is as clear as water. This is the plastic that is used to imbed biological specimens and other objects that are often seen in gift shops.

In order to obtain the flawless, glossy surface necessary for lifelike eyes, this plastic must be cast in either glass or plastic molds in which no separator is needed or used.

Hobby or handcraft shops usually carry the clear casting resin in stock. Directions for mixing with the catalyst are on the can. These stores also usually carry a large selection of plastic molds for casting all kinds of objects. If you look through these molds you can usually find some with depressions just right for casting some sizes of eyes, although they were not made for that purpose.

These stores also usually carry hollow glass balls or bulbs of various sizes which have an open neck. These are usually used for casting plastic balls, artificial grapes, and other ornaments, but when filled slightly less than half full of plastic, they are perfect for casting concave-convex eyes suitable for deer and other animals. These glass molds can be used only one time since the glass has to be broken to remove the plastic, but they are very cheap—usually about fifty cents per dozen in the correct size for making deer eyes. Fig. 76 shows some plastic molds and glass bulbs as described above.

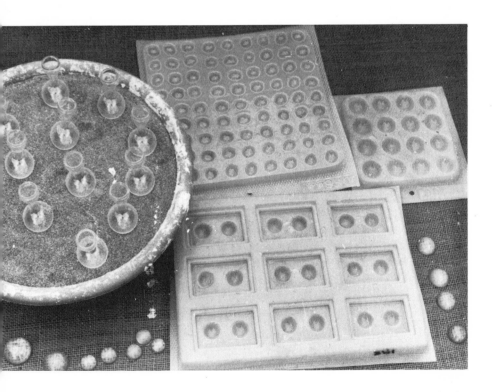

FIG. 76 Hollow glass balls and plastic molds may be used for casting artificial eyes with clear casting resin.

If you are unable to find the sizes you need in the plastic molds and glass bulbs, you can make your own as follows: Take some glass eyes of the size you want to make and lay them on a flat surface with the round side up. Cut some pieces of sheet plastic of the same type the molds are made of and lay them, glossy side down, on the eyes. These pieces of plastic should be about 3 inches in diameter or less, depending upon the size of the eyes.

Hold the plastic in place over the eye with tweezers or pliers, and with a small gas torch, heat the plastic until it begins to soften and conform to the shape of the eye. Do not keep the flame in one spot too long or the plastic will burn. Just heat it enough to make it collapse around the eye, and as you do this, take a screwdriver or some other instrument and press the plastic down around the edges of the eye so it makes close contact.

Allow the plastic to cool before touching it with your hand. You can remove the eye by pressing against the rounded part of the mold with your thumbs.

When you have your molds ready, mix some clear casting resin with the catalyst according to the directions on the can and pour it into the molds. Allow the plastic to set and cure thoroughly before removing it from the molds.

Plastic eyes cast in this manner come out very slightly concave on the back, and some can be painted just as they are. If you want to make them more concave, you can use a little power tool as shown in Fig. 77 and grind out the back as deep as you want.

On eyes which have an elongated pupil, such as the deer, you can grind out a little groove in the back of the eye, and on eyes with a round pupil you can grind a slight round depression in which to paint the pupil.

In painting eyes, several kinds of paint work quite well. You can use oil colors, but they are slow-drying, which is sometimes a disadvantage. Testor's Pla Enamel works well and dries quite fast. There are also several other paints which stick well to glass and plastic. Lacquer is good for painting the pupil and the dark rim which some eyes have around the outside edge. It dries very fast, and you can go ahead and paint the rest of the eye without having to wait a long time for these parts to dry. You can safely paint over lacquer with other paints, but do not apply lacquer over other types of paint.

FIG. 77   You can grind out the backs of plastic artificial eyes with a small power tool to make concave-convex eyes, which are best for most mammals. Such a tool can also be used to grind out a small hole or groove in which to paint the pupil.

Some eyes are definitely easier to paint than others. You might make a mess of quite a few eyes in the beginning, but the cost of making them is so low that there is no great loss. A quart of casting resin will make enough eyes to last most taxidermists for a year or more.

The easiest way to paint a round pupil is to use a small artist's brush and put a drop of black lacquer or other paint in the center of the eye. If the paint is not too thick it will naturally form a circle which is rounder than you can draw by hand. The iris of the eye can usually be painted with a brush, but in some instances it takes an airbrush to get the right effect.

Eyes painted in this manner should always be set in papier mâché, water putty, or some other water-based composition. Never set them in plastic wood or any other substance which will attack the paint. For this reason, acrylic paints should not be used in painting eyes. Acrylic paints are water-soluble, and water or almost any other liquid will affect it enough to change its color.

12

Skinning and Mounting Fish

Fish taxidermy is a phase of the work that has been sorely neglected, and even avoided, by many taxidermists. The reason for this is mostly inadequate instruction and lack of knowledge in this branch of the work. Few, if any, detailed, up-to-date instructions have been published on the basic fundamentals of doing good fish taxidermy. The few good fish taxidermists in America have gained their knowledge and skill through long years of experience and experimenting. Most of them, therefore, are understandably reluctant to share what they have learned, especially if they are in competition with others for fish work. Fish taxidermy is not easy, but it is not as difficult as many taxidermists believe it is. In this work you are working with a more or less bare skin. There is no fur or feathers to cover up mistakes; therefore, accuracy is of prime importance. One small wrinkle in a fish can spoil the appearance of what might otherwise by a beautiful mount.

There is still much to be learned and many improvements that will eventually be made in fish taxidermy. But the methods described here will adequately cover most freshwater and many saltwater species. If you live in a coastal area, however, you are almost certain to run into difficulties sooner or later. There are so many types and forms of fishes, particularly in tropical waters, that one is constantly running into new problems that must be solved as they arise. Some so-called fish taxidermists have solved most of their problems by reproducing almost all of their fish artificially and skillfully painting the replicas. It must be admitted that this system has some definite merits. It also has some disadvantages; all the patterns and colors have to be painted on the replicas and they invariably look painted. Many people do not know the difference, but many a proud fisherman would be terribly unhappy if he knew the prize fish hanging on his wall was nothing more than a painted reproduction.

Your first concern, whenever you catch or receive a fish for mounting, is to make detailed color notes. Most fish began to fade or lose some of their color almost immediately after they are taken from the water. By the time they are mounted and dried, almost all the color has either changed or disappeared completely. The spots and basic color patterns are usually still quite visible, however, which is a big help.

If you are doing commercial work, you will undoubtedly receive fish from time to time that have already lost much of their color. For this reason it is important to become familiar with all the species of fish in your locality, and to keep records and color notes of fish caught at different times of the year and sometimes in different streams and lakes in the same general area. For example, the coloration of a largemouth bass caught in a clear lake will sometimes vary considerably from one caught in a muddy stream even though the two bodies of water are close together. By the same token, a trout caught during the spawning season is usually vastly different in color from one taken at another time of the year.

A collection of color slides of freshly caught fish is sometimes very helpful when restoring the colors to a mounted fish. Color plates in books are usually not very reliable; in fact, sometimes they are totally misleading.

A handy way to take color notes of fish is shown in Fig. 78. You will notice that this chart shows the kind of fish, when and where it was caught, and gives more or less detailed notes on the coloration. Although it does not show the actual colors, it will at least remind you which colors go where. Never trust your memory on this.

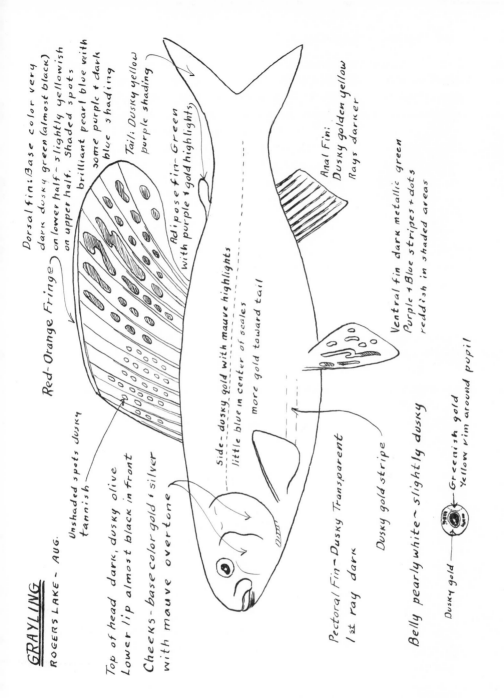

GRAYLING
ROGERS LAKE ~ AUG.

Dorsal fin: Base color very dark dusky green (almost black) on lower half ~ slightly yellowish on upper half. Shaded spots brilliant pearl blue with some purple & dark blue shading

Tail: Dusky yellow purple shading

Anal Fin: Dusky golden yellow Rays darker

Adipose fin ~ Green with purple & gold highlights)

Red-Orange Fringe

Unshaded spots dusky tannish

Top of head dark, dusky olive Lower lip almost black in front

Cheeks ~ base color gold & silver with mauve overtone

Side ~ dusky gold with mauve highlights

little blue in center of scales

more gold toward tail

Ventral fin dark metallic green Purple & Blue stripes + dots reddish in shaded areas

Pectoral Fin ~ Dusky Transparent 1st ray dark

Dusky gold stripe

Belly pearly white ~ slightly dusky

Greenish gold Yellow rim around pupil

Dusky gold

FIG. 78   A handy way of making color notes of a fish in the field. These notes are invaluable when you are restoring colors to a mounted fish.

The second step in mounting most fish is to make a plaster mold of either one side or both sides of the fish, depending upon the mounting method to be used. For this you will need a sandbox, which should be a permanent fixture in every shop. The box should be long enough to accommodate any fish you are likely to get in your area, and deep enough to hold at least 3 or 4 inches of sand.

In this chapter, four methods for mounting fish will be described, and a partial list of the types best mounted by each method will be given. These are not necessarily hard-and-fast rules. Some species can be mounted equally well by more than one method, but more often they cannot. Familiarize yourself with all these methods, and soon you will be able to tell at a glance the best method to use on almost any fish that comes to hand.

The skinning of fish, and the preparation of the mounted fish for coloring, is the same for all four methods unless otherwise noted. To avoid needless repetition, detailed instructions for doing this part of the work will be given with the first method only. For the next three methods, only the actual mounting will be described.

It is important to remember, when working on a fish, that the skin, especially the fins, should never be allowed to dry until after the fish is mounted. Keep a container of borax water handy at all times, and apply this to the skin and fins often during the skinning and mounting process.

Fish that are very slimy may be washed with water in which some alum has been dissolved. This will cut the slime and make the fish more pleasant to handle. On loose-scaled varieties, however, the slime helps to keep the scales from coming out.

SKINNING

The skinning procedure for all four methods is the same, but never start skinning the fish until you have decided which mounting method you are going to use and have made the proper molds.

Make an incision along the middle of the non-show side from the tail to the gills, cutting through the heavy shoulderbone just behind the gills. See Fig. 79.

Separate the skin from the body along the incision, cutting the membranes where necessary. Do not bend a fish skin any more

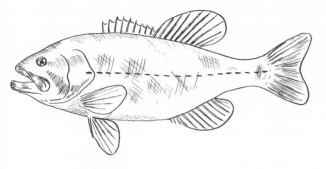

FIG. 79   The dotted line
shows where the incision
should be made in
skinning most fish.

than necessary, especially when skinning scaly fish, as you are apt
to loosen the scales.

When you have separated the skin from the body as far as
possible along the side, cut the tail free by cutting through the bone
in the base of the tail. As you reach the fins, also cut them free by
snipping the bones that hold them to the body.

Continue to cut and peel the skin from the body. Some fish skins
come off quite easily while others do not. Do not worry about
leaving quite a bit of flesh on the skin. This can be scraped off later.
Your main concern now is to get the bulk of the body out of the
skin without damaging the skin.

You will have to cut the backbone where it joins the head and
clip some bone around the gills to free the body.

At this point it is a good idea to clean up your work area. The
body may be discarded. Rinse the skin off and put it on a clean,
smooth surface.

Use a spoon or a dull knifeblade and scrape the remaining flesh
from the skin. Every particle of flesh should be removed, but try
not to scrape off the whitish or silvery lining that is present in many
fish skins.

It may be necessary to clip more bone from the base of the tail
and fins. Always remove as much bone and flesh as possible
without damaging the skin. Failure to do this is the cause of many
bad fish mounts. On some fish it is possible to run a knifeblade
down between the front and back rays of the tail and remove a little
oily flesh from that area.

Some fish such as the trout, salmon, grayling, and whitefish have a small, fleshy fin between the dorsal fin and the tail which is called the adipose fin. This fin should be opened from the inside of the skin with a small, sharp-pointed knife. Before mounting, you can squeeze a little water putty or modeling composition into this fin and shape it from the outside; otherwise, it will shrink away to almost nothing.

When you have the body skin as clean as possible, start to work on the head. This is the most difficult part of preparing a fish. It is impossible to describe an exact procedure because this varies from one fish to another. Just remember to take out all flesh and bone that you can get out without damaging the skin. A good pair of diagonal cutters or bone snips is a necessity in cleaning a fish head. Some bones must be left in the head to hold it together, but some of the bones that are left in can be trimmed down.

Be sure to open the brain cavity and remove the brain, which is small in a fish. Open up the inside of the cheeks, and remove the jaw muscles. The eyes can also be removed from the inside. Cut out the roof of the mouth and cut out as much bone and cartilage as you can from the top of the head and the nose area. Split the skin along the inside of the lower jawbones and remove the flesh from along the bone. The tongue must also be removed, but if the fish is to be mounted with open mouth it is best to leave the tongue in until the fish is mounted and almost dry. This makes it much easier to keep the shape of the head while mounting.

On some fish the skin grows directly to the bone on top of the head and cannot be separated. On others, most of the bone can be stripped off.

When you have the skin and head cleaned to your satisfaction, rinse it again in water, then apply powdered borax to all parts.

Degreasing Fish Skins: Some fish skins are very fat and oily. Such skins should never be mounted without first being degreased. If too much oil or grease is left in the skin, it will eventually work through and discolor the mounted fish. The degreasing can be done in several ways. The skin can be washed in white gasoline. This cuts the grease very well, but has a tendency to harden some fish skins. One of the best methods is to use one of the common chlorinated laundry bleaches such as Clorox or Purex. Mix 1 part of the bleach with 5 or 6 parts of water and apply this to the inside of the skin. Gently scrape the skin with a spoon or knifeblade while the bleach solution is on it. This will dissolve the grease in the skin and make it come to the surface in the form of a soapy scum. Rinse the skin in plain water after this treatment, and repeat the process if necessary. After a thorough rinsing the skin is ready for mounting. Smooth or thin-skinned fish should be rubbed inside with glycerine before mounting, but that is not necessary on fish to be mounted by Method #1, although it would do no harm.

MOUNTING BY METHOD #1

This method is very simple. It should be used for all freshwater sunfish, crappie, and small specimens of almost any scaly fish of both saltwater and freshwater varieties. It can be used on some larger specimens, but generally it is not the best method for fish more than a foot or so in length.

Decide which side of the fish is to be the show side. Scoop out a small depression in the sand and lay the fish in the depression with the show side up. Arrange it in the position wanted. Push the sand up around the specimen so that only the top half is exposed. See Fig. 80.

Mix up some molding or casting plaster to a thick, creamy consistency and apply this to the fish. The entire exposed half of the body should be covered except the end of the tail and the front end of the head, as shown in Fig. 79.

After the first coat of plaster has been applied, you can dip patches of burlap in the plaster and lay these on the mold to strengthen it. The mold should be made quite strong for this method.

When the mold has completely hardened, turn it over and take the fish out. Wash the sand and any plaster residue off the fish and it is ready to be skinned.

Place the skin in the half-mold that you made previously. Make sure that all parts fit into the corresponding places in the mold. Mix up some fish mix, Formula #13 in the Appendix, to a very thick, doughlike consistency and press it firmly into all parts of the skin. Be sure that the base of the tail and the base of the fins are well filled. Pack the head full of the mix, making sure that the cheeks are well filled.

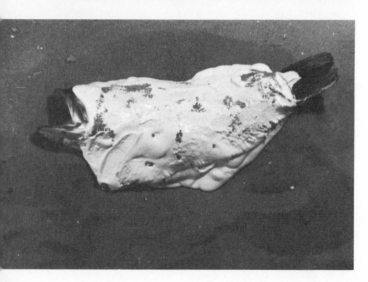

FIG. 80   A bass in the sand box in preparation for making a mold, and the same fish with the mold poured of the show side.

On very small fish the skin may be completely filled with the fish mix except for a little block of wood which is imbedded on the back side to fasten a hanger to later. On the larger specimens to be mounted by this method, it may be desirable to place a lightweight core of some kind inside the body to reduce the weight of the finished mount. If this is to be done, you can use a core of balsa wood, styrofoam, or almost any lightweight material, but be sure there is a quarter-inch or so of fish mix between the core and the skin on the show side. Also, be sure to leave enough room on the back side to insert a small piece of plywood so that a hanger can be attached later. This block of wood should be large enough to accommodate the hanger and should be placed so it will be sure to cover the center of gravity or balance point on the fish.

When the hanger block is installed, finish filling any open areas and pull the skin so the two edges fit together.

It is not always necessary to sew up the incision on very small fish, but the larger ones should be sewn.

It is necessary to work fairly fast when filling a fish by this method so you will get through before the fish mix starts to set up.

After the fish is filled and the incision closed, hold a piece of flexible cardboard against the fish so that it makes contact from head to tail. Place your other hand under the mold and turn the whole thing over so the fish is lying on the cardboard. The cardboard should be a little longer and wider than the fish. Place blocks of wood or wads of paper under the ends of the cardboard to support the head and tail if the fish is mounted in a curve. The plaster mold may then be lifted off.

If the fish mix has not yet set up, you can alter the curve of the fish slightly if it needs to be altered, but be very careful not to make any dents or impressions in the body.

Carding the Fins: Your next step is to card the fins. Dip your fingers in water and wet the fins until they are completely relaxed and pliable. For carding, you can use strips of cardboard or thin strips of balsa wood. The latter is preferable because it allows evaporation without sticking to the fins as cardboard sometimes does. Spread out each fin and put a strip of cardboard or balsa wood on the front and back of the fins. These strips can be held together with paperclips on small fish or spring-type clothespins on larger fish. Wads of paper or some other support will be needed to hold the carded fins in the correct position until they are dry. See Fig. 81.

Allow the fish to dry thoroughly. This will take from a few days to a few weeks, depending upon the size and kind of fish and the weather conditions. The drying time can be speeded up considerably by placing the fish near a stove in cold weather or outside in

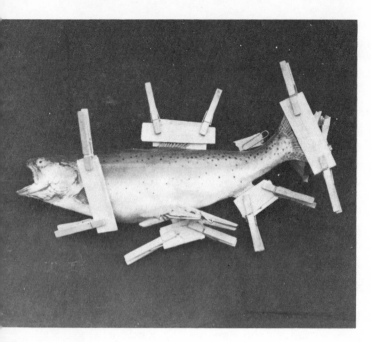

FIG. 81   A mounted fish with fins spread and carded. The strips of balsa are good for carding; they allow evaporation without sticking to the fins as cardboard often does.

warm weather. Be careful not to let the fish become too hot either from artificial heat or from the sun. Too much heat is likely to make the scales curl up on some fish, and also to cause excessive shrinkage in the skin.

When the fins and tail are completely dry, the strips may be taken off the fins. As soon as this is done, the fins should be backed with clear plastic. The dry fins are very fragile, and the plastic backing strengthens them and also patches any split places or ragged edges. Mylar is excellent for backing fins, but you can use any clear sheet plastic that is moderately stiff and not too thick.

Cut out pieces of the plastic a little larger than the fins and tail. Use the clearest contact cement that you can get, and apply a coat of this to the back of each fin and the tail. Also, apply a coat to the front side of each piece of plastic.

Allow the contact cement to dry thoroughly to the touch, then apply the plastic to the back of the fins. Be very careful to get it correctly placed on the first attempt because once the two cemented surfaces are in contact with each other the plastic cannot easily be removed without damage to the fin. Press the fin and plastic firmly together with your fingers to make certain that good contact is made. You may then trim the plastic with scissors or a razor blade.

Setting the Glass Eyes: You can set the glass eyes immediately after the fish is mounted or wait until it is dry if you prefer. On fish which are to be hung on the wall, only one eye is generally used, since the other one would not show anyway.

Glass eyes for fish can be bought already colored for some species, or you can buy clear eyes with only the pupil painted. These are to be hand-painted as needed. If you do much fish work it is usually preferable, and much cheaper, to get the clear eyes and paint them yourself.

Most fish eyes have either a gold or silver iris with small specks or blotches of black or other color scattered throughout. Use a small pointed brush and paint the specks on the back of the eye first. When this is dry, paint the whole back of the eye with gold, silver, or a combination of the two as should be recorded on your color notes.

If the filling in the eye cavity is still soft when you are ready to set the eye, just press the glass eye in place. If the filling has hardened, dig out enough to make room for the eye plus a little fresh papier mâché to set the eye in.

Modeling the Mouth: If the fish is mounted with the mouth open, as they usually are, the inside of the mouth must be modeled in. This should be done after the fish is dry or almost dry.

If you have not previously removed the tongue, this should be done now. The tongue can be clipped out with diagonal cutters or strong shears, and the remaining flesh under the tongue scraped out with a spoon.

On fish mounted by Method #1, with a completely filled body, just put a little water putty or modeling compound in the mouth cavity and model it into shape. It can be smoothed out with a soft brush dipped in water.

On fish mounted by one of the other methods, with a hollow body, you can place a wad of paper down in the throat area and then model the mouth in the same manner. Ordinarily, very little detail modeling is done in the mouth, as this adds little or nothing to the appearance of the fish. In special cases, however, where exact detail is desired, you can make an impression of the mouth of the fresh fish with dental impression material and cast it in acrylic plastic or some other material and set it in the fish during the mounting process.

Attaching the Hanger: When the fish is dry and the mouth has been modeled in, a hanger should be attached to the back side. To make the fish hang level, you must place the hanger on the center of gravity, or point of balance, between the head and tail. To find this point, place the fish on the edge of a board or some other narrow object and make a mark at the point where the fish balances. See Fig. 82.

FIG. 82   Find the balance point on a mounted fish so that you can position the hanger properly.

It usually looks better to have the fish stand out from the wall a little. To do this, attach a small block of wood to the back of the fish with screws and attach the hanger to this block.

If the fish is to be put on a wall panel or shield, it is attached to this in the same way, but not until the fish has been colored and

FIG. 83 A small bream and crappie mounted by Method #1.

finished. If mounted on a panel, the balance point must be located on the back of the panel after the fish is attached.

MOUNTING BY METHOD # 2

This is sometimes called the sock method. It is similar to Method #1, but is better adapted to larger fish. This method is excellent for bass, pike, muskellunge, gar, sturgeon, the larger perch, carp, and many saltwater varieties such as the mangrove snapper, red snapper, dog snapper, muttonfish, bonefish, tarpon shad, jewfish, grouper, cod, tautog, puddingwife, parrotfish, channel bass, black drum, snook, barracuda, and dolphin, and also many others.

The first step in this method is to make an outline drawing of your fish. Lay the fish on a sheet of paper with the show side up. Trace the outline of the body only. Do not include the projecting fins and tail fin. This outline is eventually to become a pattern from which to make a cloth bag, or sock, to be filled with sawdust or sand and temporarily used inside the fish as a partial filler or core. This bag, when finished, should be the same general shape as the fish but enough smaller to have approximately three-eighths to one-half inch of space between the sock and the skin on all sides. In order to accomplish this you will have to adjust the size of your pattern according to the thickness of the fish.

Measure the circumference of the fish at the smallest part. Suppose this measurement is 8 inches. Measure the diameter of the corresponding place on your outline. Suppose this is 3 inches. This means that the circumference of the sock at this point would be 6 inches as compared to 8 inches on the fish. Allowing a little for the thickness of the skin, this would not leave quite enough space between the sock and the skin, so the pattern should be cut down a little at this point. Make marks on the pattern to show how much it should be reduced.

Now, let us take another example. Suppose the circumference of your fish is 20 inches around the middle, and the diameter on your outline is 6 inches. This would mean that the circumference of the sock would be 12 inches as compared to 20 inches on the fish. This would leave far too much space between the sock and the skin, so the pattern will have to be enlarged in the middle. Put marks outside your original outline to indicate this.

Another measurement should be taken just back of the head and the results of your finding marked on the pattern in the same manner.

Without getting into mathematical problems, an easy way to determine the size your pattern should be is to cut a small wire the length of each circumference measurement on the fish. Bend these wires into a circle. With another piece of wire, form another circle inside the first, leaving three-eighths to one-half inch between the two circles. Half the length of the inner wire will be the correct diameter for your pattern. See Fig. 84.

When the correct dimensions have been determined, re-outline the pattern to conform with the necessary changes. At the front end of your pattern, in the head area, let the lines flare out into a funnel shape as shown in Fig. 83. This will make it easier to fill the sock with sawdust or sand. It is also a good idea to put a mark of some kind on the pattern to show which is the show side.

When this is done, cut the pattern out and lay it, show side up, on two thicknesses of cloth. Then carefully mark the outline on the cloth. The top layer of cloth should also be marked to show that it is the show side.

Sew the two pieces of cloth together along the pattern line, but leave the funnel end open. Cut the excess cloth off just outside your stitches.

A small block of plywood should be placed inside the sock and stapled or tacked to the back or bottom piece of cloth. This block is to receive the hanger screws later, so be sure it is big enough to cover the balance point on the fish. If the funnel end is quite small, you may have to put the block in before the sock is sewn up.

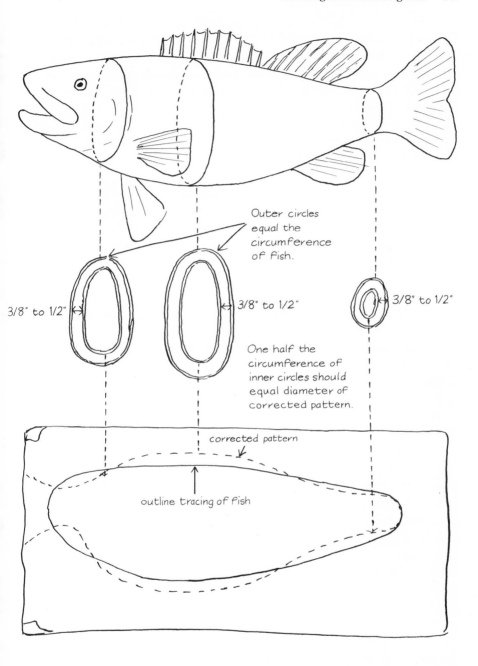

Outer circles equal the circumference of fish.

3/8" to 1/2"

3/8" to 1/2"

3/8" to 1/2"

One half the circumference of inner circles should equal diameter of corrected pattern.

corrected pattern

outline tracing of fish

FIG. 84   This sketch shows the easiest procedure for making a sock to mount a fish by Method #2.

Fill the sock with sawdust or sand, and pack it as tightly as possible. Sand is all right on small fish, but sawdust should be used on the larger fish because it is not so heavy. When the sock is full, tie it securely with string around the small part of the funnel. See Fig. 85.

A mold is made of the show side of the fish just as described in Method #1. The fish is also skinned and treated exactly as described in the first method. When the skin is ready to be mounted, lay it in the mold so that all parts fit correctly. Line the show side with layer of fish mix, Formula #13. The fish mix should be mixed to a thick, doughlike consistency and packed firmly against the skin to a depth of three-eighths to one-half inch. This layer should cover all parts of the skin that is in the mold.

Place the filled sock in the skin with the funnel end in the fish's mouth. Press the sock down firmly against the layer of fish mix; then put a layer of the mix on top of the sock. Pull the edges of the skin together, and if they can be made to overlap, add a little more of the fish mix until the edges come together perfectly.

The most important point to remember in this process is to pack the fish mix firmly. Do not be afraid to push and pound on it, but not hard enough to break the mold underneath.

When the edges of the skin meet properly, sew up the incision, starting from the tail end. The fish and mold may now be turned over on a piece of cardboard as described for Method #1. Make any minor changes needed in the position of the body, and put cardboard or balsa-wood strips on the fins as already described.

The fish should now be set aside to dry. When it is thoroughly dry, the hanger may be attached to the back side. In this method you have to guess where the center of gravity will be because the mouth has not yet been modeled in and the sawdust is still inside. The hanger, however, should be attached before the sawdust is emptied rather than taking a chance of crushing the fish while putting the screws in the back.

After the hanger has been attached, the sawdust filling may be emptied. To do this, reach into the mouth with a sharp knife and cut off the funnel of the sock.

With a stiff wire or small rod, probe the sawdust and empty it as it is loosened. Do not try to remove the cloth sock; it helps to strengthen the fish, and it is held in by the wooden hanger block

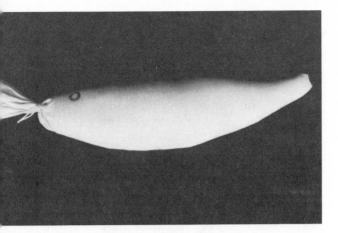

FIG. 85   A finished cloth sock filled with sawdust. The eye has been marked on the sock.

FIG. 86   A bass mounted by Method #2.

anyway. With the sawdust removed the fish will finish drying out much more rapidly.

When the fish is thoroughly dry inside, place a wad of paper in the throat and model the mouth as previously described.

Fish mounted by this method can be easily crushed if you remove the sawdust too soon. After they are thoroughly dry and cured, however, they are very light and durable.

MOUNTING BY METHOD #3

This is called the hard-body method. It should be used for all trout, salmon, grayling, and all smooth-skinned varieties such as catfish, mackeral, bonita, tuna, cobia, and others.

In using this method a mold is made of both sides of the fish. Place the fish in the sandbox and arrange it in exactly the position you want. This is very important because the position of a fish mounted by this method cannot be altered after the body is made. Arrange the sand around the fish so that only the top half is exposed. Make a plaster mold of this side as described earlier. This mold should cover the entire side of the fish from the eye to the base of the tail.

When the first half of the mold has hardened thoroughly, carefully turn the mold over without removing the fish. Trim the edges of the mold with a sharp knife, being careful not to cut the fish. Wash off any sand from the fish or the edge of the mold and grease the edge of the mold with stearine or some other separator. When this is done, proceed to make the other half of the mold.

When the second half of the mold has thoroughly hardened, carefully pry the mold apart and remove the fish.

The fish should next be washed, skinned, and prepared for mounting as described for Method #1.

When the skin has been taken care of, the artificial body can be made. Brush any sand from the inside of the mold and fill any large bubble holes with plaster. The impressions and holes left by the fins should also be filled level and smoothed over. The entire head area of the mold should not only be smoothed over, it should be built up about one-eighth to one-quarter inch. Follow the line of the gill covers and build up from there forward.

When the patching and altering has hardened, wet the entire mold with water. Mix up a little fresh plaster, very thin, and quickly paint this over the entire inner surface of the mold, filling up any scale prints and making the surface as smooth as possible.

Allow the mold to dry for a while; then give it a coat of shellac on the inside. When the shellac is dry, cut two pieces of burlap to fit inside each piece of the mold. These pieces should be large enough to cover the entire inner surface of the mold and project an inch or so beyond the edges.

Paint the shellacked surface of the mold with stearine, being very careful not to miss any spots.

Next, mix up some molding plaster to a thin, creamy consistency. Dip a piece of the burlap into the plaster, making sure that it is thoroughly saturated. As you lift the burlap, strip off some of the excess plaster, and lay the burlap in the mold. With a paintbrush, quickly and firmly brush out the entire surface so that there are no air spaces between the burlap and the mold. Wash out your brush before the plaster sets in it. Then put in the second layer of burlap in the same manner.

Repeat the process on the other half of the mold.

On very large fish, three layers of burlap may be needed, but two layers will ordinarily be sufficient on fish up to 3 feet long, although an extra strip can be used on the back side where the hanger block will be.

The hanger block can be a piece of waterproof plywood. It should be about one-third the length of the body and should be placed about in the middle of the back side of the form. It can be held in place by putting a strip or two of burlap and plaster over it.

When the form has hardened, take a sharp knife and trim the edges even with the edge of the mold. Always cut against the mold instead of away from it and you will get a cleaner cut.

After the edges have been trimmed, the form may be removed from the mold. If the mold was properly coated with stearine, the form will come out easily.

Fit the two halves of the form together and do any slight trimming needed to make them fit properly. To fasten the two pieces together, spread a thin layer of plaster along the edge of half of the form and quickly put the pieces together. Tie each end of the form securely with string until the plaster has hardened. You can also put a little plaster in the tail area and little strips of burlap and plaster over the seams in the front end as far as you can reach. Examine the surface of the form and fill any bubble holes or flaws. Make the form as smooth as possible over the entire surface. See Fig. 87.

Allow the form to dry completely. Artificial heat may be used to speed up the drying if you are in a hurry.

After the form is dry, it can be sanded with medium sandpaper to smooth any rough spots. It should then be given two or three coats of shellac before the skin is put on.

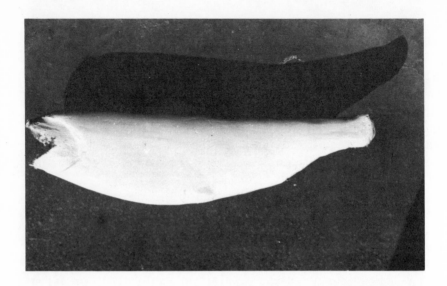

FIG. 87   A hard body for a fish to be
mounted by Method #3. This body is
made of plaster and burlap, but they can
be made of fiberglass or laminated paper.

NOTE: When Method #3 is used on small fish under a foot or so
in length, a fiberglass form is better. Fiberglass can be used on any
size fish for that matter, but it is much more expensive than plaster-
and-burlap and perhaps a little harder to use.

Laminated paper forms can also be used, but are much slower.

When you are ready to mount the fish, examine the skin again
and make sure it is clean and smooth inside. Since most fish
mounted by this method are rather thin-skinned, and the skin is
being mounted on a hard body, additional care is needed to see that
the skin is perfectly clean inside. Any particle as large as a grain of
sand trapped under the skin will show up plainly on the mounted
fish.

Rinse the skin in plain water to remove the excess powdered
borax and to thoroughly relax the skin. If the fish has an adipose
fin, do not forget to open it up from the inside and force a little
water putty into it.

With paper towels, blot the excess water from the inside of the skin, then rub the inside of the skin with glycerine. This will keep it from drying too fast and will also prevent it from cracking.

Put a little water putty in the base of the tail and fins and place the skin on the form. Holding the skin in position, turn the form over and sew up the incision, starting from the tail. As you sew, keep checking to see that the skin does not slip out of place. Be sure that the dorsal fin is in the right place on the back.

When the incision is closed, turn the fish back over. Fill the cheek areas with papier mâché, fish mix, or water putty. Fill out the head as much as necessary with the filling and model it into shape. If necessary, you can wrap the head with a few turns of gauze or strips of cloth to hold the gill covers down and to hold the head in shape. Do not wind it tight enough to make indentations in the skin.

The fins and tail should next be spread and carded with strips of balsa wood or cardboard as previously described. When this is done, allow the fish to dry. The eyes may be set at any time, but the mouth should not be modeled in until the fish is dry. Also, the hanger should not be attached until the fins are backed and the mouth modeled in; these additions in weight will change the center of gravity.

FIG. 88   A trout mounted by Method #3.

MOUNTING A FISH BY METHOD #3, START TO FINISH

Following is a step-by-step pictorial guide to skinning and mounting a fish by Method #3. The subject here is a 32-inch, 15-pound Dolly Varden, but these instructions apply to any fish to be mounted by this method. The skinning and preparation of the skin is basically the same for most fish regardless of the mounting method used.

If the fish is very slimy you can wash it with alum water to remove fish just after it was caught.

If the fish is very slimy you can wash it with alum water to remove the slime and make it more pleasant to handle.

1 Place the fish in the sand box in the position you want the finished mount. It should be half buried in the sand from head to tail. The pectoral fin can be tied in an upright position as shown here or allowed to lie flat against the body.

2 Mix a bowl of molding or casting plaster to a creamy consistency and apply a coat of plaster from the eye to the tail.

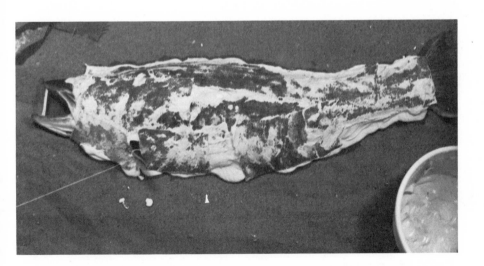

3 Have some strips of burlap ready. Dip these in the remaining plaster and lay them on the fish over the first coat of plaster. This will reinforce the mold. Two layers of the burlap strips should make the mold strong enough.

4 When the first half of the mold has thoroughly hardened, carefully turn it over, keeping the fish in the mold. Wash or scrape the sand from the fish and trim the edge of the mold fairly smooth with a sharp knife.

5 Paint the trimmed edges of the mold with stearine, petroleum jelly, or some other good separator so the second half of the mold will not stick to the first.

6 Make a mold of the other side in the same manner that you made the first half. The fish is now completely encased in plaster except for the front of the head and the end of the tail.

7 When the second half of the mold has hardened, pry the two halves apart and remove the fish. Wash it in running water to remove any plaster residue that is on the skin. Lay the mold aside for the time being.

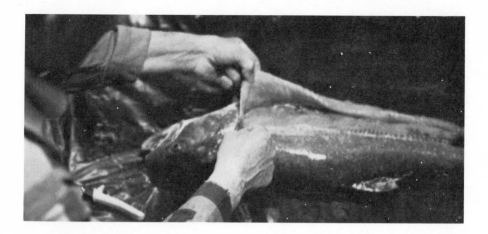

8 To skin the fish, make an incision on the back side from the tail to the gill opening. Snip the heavy shoulder bone that lies just under the edge of the gill opening and cut in both directions around this bone.

9 Peel the skin back on each side of the body incision. Cut the pectoral and ventral fins loose from the body and expose the entire half of the body as shown. You can now cut the dorsal, anal, and tail fins loose. The backbone should also be severed from the skull at this time. You can now skin the other side of the body.

10 This shows the skin completely removed from the body. You can now dispose of the body and start cleaning the skin.

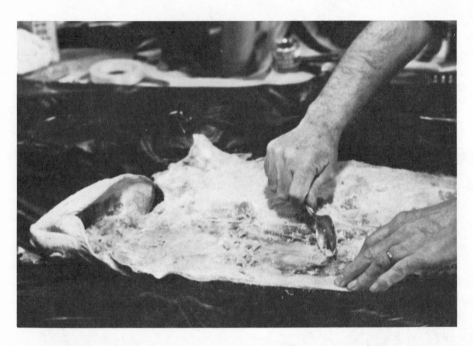

11 A tablespoon is one of the best tools for scraping the skin. On most fish it is best to scrape from the tail end toward the head. The ends of the fin and tail bones should be clipped down as close to the skin as possible. The head is the most troublesome part of the fish to clean. The best rule to follow here is to take out all the flesh and as much bone as you can without destroying the framework of the head. The eyes and cheek muscles are removed from the inside. Much of the bone in the top of the head can be removed, but it is best to leave the tongue intact until the fish is mounted.

12 When the skin is cleaned, rinse it in water and apply plenty of borax to both the inside and outside. It should then be placed in a plastic bag and kept in refrigeration until you are ready to mount it.

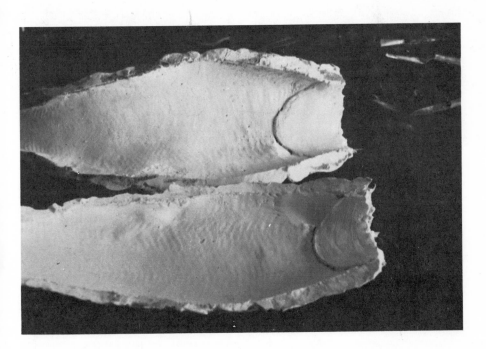

13 You can now turn your attention back to the mold. The imprint left by the gill covers should be built up with plaster about ¼ inch higher than the body surface of the mold. Any holes or imprints left by the fins should also be filled in and smoothed over.

14 Mix a little plaster quite thin and brush this over the entire inner surface of the mold, making it as smooth as possible. This coat of plaster should be built up thick enough to compensate for the thickness of the skin. Allow this to dry for an hour or so and then give the inside of the mold two coats of shellac or clear lacquer. When this is dry, apply a coat of stearine or some other good separator.

15 Cut out two pieces of burlap to fit in each piece of the mold, allowing about an inch overhang on all sides.

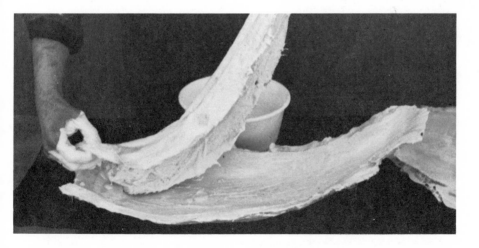

16 Mix some plaster to a rather thin creamy consistency. Dip the pieces of burlap in the plaster one at a time and put two pieces in each half of the mold. Each piece should be well pressed down and smoothed out in the mold before the next piece is put in.

17 Put a block of plywood in the back, or wall side, of the form and fasten it down with strips of burlap dipped in plaster. This block is to receive the screws for the hanger which will be put on the mounted fish. It should be centered where you estimate the center of gravity or balance point will be. This is usually a little forward of the middle of the form.

18 When the form has hardened, use a sharp knife and trim the edges even with the edge of the mold.

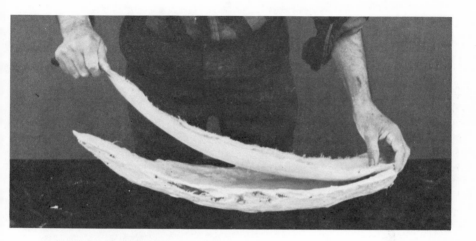

19 The pieces of the form can easily be removed from the mold by prying along the edge with a knife blade.

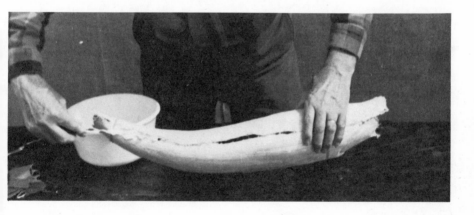

20 Dab a little plaster along the edge of one piece of the form and fit the two pieces together. Any gaps in the seam can be filled with plaster and smoothed over. Small strips of burlap and plaster can also be put over the seam inside as far down in the open end as you can reach. Any dents or depressions in the body over which the skin might "drumhead" as it dries should be filled with plaster and smoothed over with a brush dipped in water. When the form is finished, allow it to dry thoroughly. You can greatly speed up the drying by leaving it out in the sunshine in warm weather or by putting it on a warm heater.

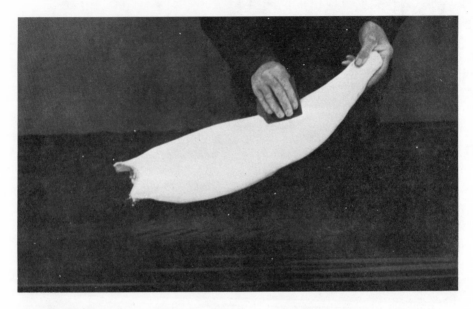

21 When the form is completely dry, any rough spots should be sanded smooth with coarse sandpaper. It should then be given at least two coats of shellac or clear lacquer. When that is dry you can go ahead with the mounting.

22 Rinse the skin thoroughly in water to remove all the borax from the surface. Check it carefully to see that no bits of flesh or foreign matter remain on the skin. If the skin seems oily it should be degreased. To do this, mix 4 or 5 parts of water with 1 part of any chlorinated laundry bleach such as Clorox or Purex. Pour a little of this mixture on the flesh side of the skin and scrape with a knife blade or a spoon. The oil will come to the surface in the form of a soapy scum. Rinse the skin again to remove the bleach solution. Immediately before mounting the skin, pour a little glycerin on the flesh side and rub it well into all parts with your fingers. This will prevent the skin from drying too fast and possibly prevent it from cracking later.

23 Try the skin on the form and check to see that there are no irregularities that need to be corrected. A little papier mâché or water putty may be needed in the base of the tail and fins. If you use water putty for this, add a little vinegar to the water to retard the setting time.

24 Turn the fish over and start sewing the incision at the tail end. Check often to see that the fins are in the right position on the body. When you reach the head, fill the cheek area with papier mâché or water putty and put a little under the gill cover. The gill cover on that side may be stapled down to hold it in place. Turn the fish over and finish modeling the head on the show side. A strip of cloth may be wrapped around the head if necessary to hold everything in place, but it should not be tight enough to leave an impression.

25 The fins and tail should now be spread and carded with strips of stiff cardboard or balsa wood. The latter is better since it does not stick to the fins as much as cardboard. The strips can be held in place with clothespins or large paper clips. Before doing this it is best to lay the fish on a board so it can be moved from one location to another without disturbing the fins. Use wads of paper, small sticks, or any means necessary to support the fins in the correct position until they are dry and stiff.

26 When the fins are dry they are quite fragile. To remedy this they should be backed with clear sheet plastic of moderate stiffness such as mylar. Cut pieces of the plastic slightly larger than each fin. Apply a coat of contact cement to the back of each fin and the front surface of each piece of plastic. Allow the cement to dry and then carefully place the plastic on the fin. Be sure to get the plastic in the right position on the first attempt. When the two cemented surfaces come in contact the plastic cannot usually be removed without damaging the fin. Trim the overhang carefully with scissors or a razor blade.

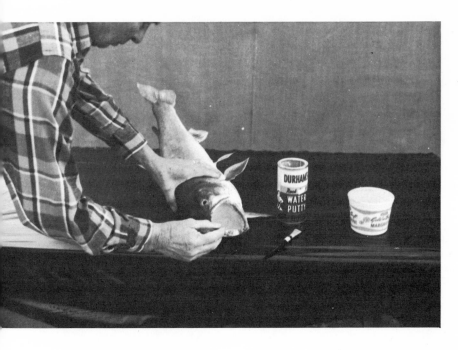

27 When the fish is dry, or almost so, the tongue may be removed by cutting around the lower jaw just inside the mouth and by clipping the bones on each side that support the tongue. The fleshy area under the tongue can be scraped out with a spoon. Allow the mouth to dry more if needed. This picture shows the mouth being modeled in. To do this, stuff a wad of paper into the throat area and model the mouth with water putty. When it begins to harden it can be smoothed with a brush dipped in water. The artificial eyes may also be set at this time in a bed of water putty.

28 Now that all appreciable weight has been added to the fish you can attach the hanger to the back side. To do this you must first find the center of gravity or balance point so the fish will hang level.

You can easily find this point by balancing the fish on the edge of a board as shown here. Make a small mark on the fish on each side of the board and place the hanger between the two marks.

29 The hanger is attached to the fish with screws which extend into the block of wood inside the fish.

30 When the fish is completely dry it should be given a coat of shellac which has been thinned a little with alcohol. If any smoothing or patchwork is needed about the head, this can be done with plastic wood or automobile body putty. Either of these can be sanded smooth when dry and then shellacked again. The fish is then ready to be colored. Directions for coloring are given elsewhere in this chapter. This picture shows the fish being colored with an airbrush, which is far superior to brush painting in most cases. Small spots and stripes, however, can sometimes be handled best with an artist's brush.

31 The finish coats of clear lacquer are being applied with a paint sprayer. The first coat should be applied rather sparingly. This will set the colors and prevent them from running. When the first coat is dry to touch, the second coat can be applied more heavily, but not thick enough to start running or sagging. At least three coats should be applied in all.

32 The finished fish.

MOUNTING BY METHOD #4

This method is rather crude and is rarely used except on a few saltwater species on which a suitable mold cannot be made because of their physical structure. Some of the swellfish, such as the rabbitfish, come in this category. Such fish as the sargassum, toadfish, and scorpionfish may also be mounted by this method.

This method consists of taking careful measurements of the body, then making an excelsior form in the same way that a bird body is made except with a wooden core. The form should be made slightly small and modeled over with papier mâché or water putty to make it the correct size. The form is inserted in the skin and filled out with papier mâché where necessary. The specimen is dried and finished in the same way as in the previous methods.

The swellfish, such as the rabbitfish, can be inflated by shooting compressed air into the anus. They will usually remain inflated long enough to take the necessary measurements, or they can be reinflated as many times as necessary.

MOUNTING SAILFISH AND MARLIN

Some fish, such as the sailfish and marlin, are so constructed that it is impossible to skin and mount them properly by any of the methods described above.

On these fish there is a deep groove down the center of the back which the large dorsal fin grows out of and can fold into.

The skin on the sides is covered with small, tight scales and is quite tough and easily skinned. The skin along the back and belly, however, is very thin, oily, and rather fibrous; it is almost impossible to prepare for mounting. Furthermore, a taxidermist rarely receives a sailfish on which the sail is not ripped to shreds.

For these reasons, the usual practice is to use only certain parts of the original fish and to reconstruct the rest artificially. Fortunately, this is not as difficult as it might seem.

A mold can easily be made of the two sides. The dorsal fin acts as a natural partition along most of the back, and a strip of cardboard can be inserted in the groove along the belly to form a partition part of the distance there. The fish should, of course, be posed in the desired position first.

If you make a good mold with sharp detail, and make a good plaster and burlap cast from the mold, you can use this for the body and not use the skin at all if you wish. The tail and all the fins except the long, slender ventral fins can be dried and attached to the cast when the two halves are being put together. The anal fin and the small fin on the back behind the sail are usually made artificially, however, since they are quite fleshy and are subject to shrinkage. The large dorsal fin, or sail, and the long, slender ventral fins are almost always made artificially. These are also attached before the two sides are put together. The natural head can be cleaned, degreased, and attached last. This is easily done on a sailfish because the head is almost a separate unit and can be placed on the body almost like putting on a hat. Only a small area

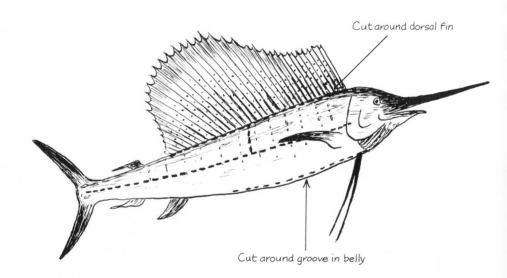

Cut around dorsal fin

Cut around groove in belly

FIG. 89   The dotted lines show the cuts to be made to skin a sailfish if you want to use the entire skin.

across the back of the head will have to be blended in with the rest of the body.

Sometimes only the scaly side portions of the skin are used. These pieces can be securely glued to the cast after sanding it off, or they can be placed in the mold and incorporated with the cast.

The entire skin, or most of it, can be used if you wish, but it is generally not satisfactory to do so. Fig. 89 shows the incisions to make in a sailfish if you want to use the entire skin.

The large dorsal fin can be made in several ways. Ordinarily it is made of tempered Masonite or hardboard.

The first step in making the dorsal fin, or sail, is to establish the back curve of the fish. This is done by laying the show side of your cast on the hardboard and tracing the outline of the back the entire distance the sail will cover. Allow a few inches of hardboard at the bottom to extend down into the body of the fish. See Fig. 90.

The rays of the fin can be represented by gluing small, tapered

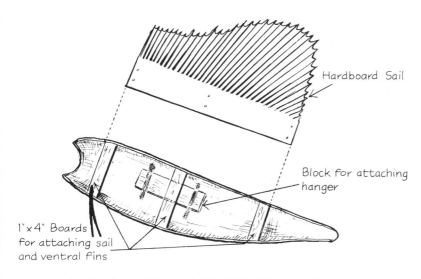

Hardboard Sail

Block for attaching hanger

1"x 4" Boards for attaching sail and ventral fins

Inside View of Back Half of Sailfish Manikin

FIG. 90   Inside view of back half of a sailfish manikin, showing how the sail assembly is attached.

strips to the hardboard. The original bony rays of the fin can be cleaned and used if you wish, but other materials are less trouble and generally look better. If you can get palm fronds, excellent strips can be made from them. They are already tapered, and are light, tough, and easy to work with.

When the arrangement and curve of the rays has been established, the outline of the fin is drawn and carefully sawed out. The fin should be kept very smooth and neat; any flaws will appear to be magnified many times when the fish is finished.

Apply several coats of shellac to the fin after the rays have been glued on. Sand each coat of shellac lightly with fine sandpaper after it has dried. This will make a good base for the final finish.

The long, slender ventral fins are best made of sheet metal. They are so long and slender toward the end that any other material is apt to be broken.

A block of wood must be set in the back half of the cast for attaching a hanger. Other pieces of wood should also be installed for attaching the dorsal and ventral fins. See Fig. 87. When these two artificial fins have been attached, the other fins and tail can be attached, and the two halves put together. The head is put on last.

After the body is assembled, do any patching and smoothing that is necessary, and when all is dry, apply at least one coat of shellac to all parts. It is then ready to be colored.

MOUNTING SHARKS AND RELATED SPECIES

No method has yet been perfected by which the sharks, rays, sawfish, etc. can be mounted with complete success. They can be mounted in the same manner as other fish, but because of the cartilaginous nature of the fins and the structure of the head, the results are usually far from satisfactory.

The simplest and most logical way to handle such creatures is to make a mold of the entire body in as many pieces as necessary, then make a cast in reinforced plaster or fiberglass. The cast can then be painted in natural colors as you would finish any other fish. The natural teeth can be used in the cast if they are to show.

A porpoise is a mammal rather than a fish, but it is similar to the sharks in structure. Fig. 59 shows a freshwater porpoise cast in fiberglass as just described.

COLORING AND FINISHING FISH

The coloring and finishing of mounted fish is one of the most important aspects of the work. A well-mounted fish that is improperly colored, or has a yellow varnish finish, is not a very attractive sight.

For many years, fish were almost invariably painted with oil colors and finished with a coat or two of varnish. A large percentage of commercial taxidermists still use this method, but the airbrush and the use of dyes and lacquer or plastic finishes have long since made this technique obsolete.

For one who does, or expects to do, only a small amount of fish mounting, the purchase of an air compressor, airbrush, and paint sprayer may seem like a poor investment; but once you have this equipment in your shop it would be hard to get along without it. Many uses can be found for an air compressor, and an airbrush is unequaled for finishing the nose, mouth, eyelids, etc. of mounted heads.

It would be quite impossible to describe the exact procedure for coloring fish, because this varies somewhat with each species, and to some extent with each fish. The first important step, however, is to see that the surface of your fish is smooth and free from cracks and blemishes. Sometimes little bumps and depressions appear on the fish's head because of shrinkage in drying. Any such places should be modeled over and made perfectly smooth before coloring and finishing the fish. The fiberglass putty used to repair dents in automobile fenders works quite well for this. Plastic wood can also be used with good results.

After all patching is done, give the patched area at least one good coat of shellac and let it dry thoroughly. If the area still looks a little rough and has a different texture from the rest of the head, you can apply a coat of fiberglass resin to the smooth portions of the head, but do not put it on any scaly areas. When using this resin in small amounts you can add a little more catalyst than the directions call for and make it set up faster. When it is dry, give it a coat of shellac, and if the entire body of the fish has not yet been shellacked, give it a coat also.

Many fish have highly iridescent, or pearly, areas on the body. Such fish should be given a light coat of essence of pearl with your airbrush, applying it only to the areas where the iridescence should be, and heavier where the iridescence is strongest. This coat of pearl will not be highly visible at this time.

Essence of pearl is usually sold in liquid or paste form and is thinned with lacquer thinner before using. It is more compatible with some brands of lacquer thinner than it is with others. Try a small amount first, and if it does not mix smoothly and easily, try another brand of lacquer thinner. It should be mixed quite thin for airbrush work.

The colors which should appear in the iridescent areas are applied over the pearl base. The color should usually be applied very sparingly, because it does not show up as much when first applied as it will after the finish coat is applied. Very strong iridescent effects can be gotten by mixing colors, either lacquer or dyes, with a little essence of pearl.

The back and upper sides of a fish are usually darker than the rest of the body, and usually have some highlights which disappear during drying. These highlights can usually be restored by spraying dye of the proper color over the area.

If you have had to do patchwork on the head or other areas, the color must usually be applied quite heavily over these areas to hide the patches.

On many fish, the fins are quite transparent, or semi-transparent, and should remain that way. The colors in these fins, therefore, should be restored with dyes rather than highly pigmented paint. Some fish, however, have such brightly colored and heavily pigmented markings on the fins that these areas must be painted to achieve the desired effect.

As a general rule, it is preferable to do as much of the coloring as you can with your airbrush. Fish which have small specks or definite lines to be painted should have the airbrush work done first, and then the specks and lines painted by hand with a small sable-hair brush.

After all the coloring is done, it usually improves the appearance of the fish to use black lacquer in your airbrush and do a little shading along the back and head and around the mouth.

For a final finish, use the best clear gloss lacquer that you can get, and thin it according to the manufacturer's recommendations for spray work. Do not use this in your airbrush but rather in a paint sprayer with a quart container which can be attached to your air compressor. Two or three nozzles usually come with a paint spray outfit. The one which sprays in a fan shape is usually best for spraying fish.

The first coat of the clear lacquer should cover the fish well, but not be applied too heavily. Let this coat dry to touch. This will set the colors and prepare the fish for the next coat. Apply the second coat quite heavily so the fish definitely looks wet, but always keep the spray moving. Never spray in one place long enough to make the lacquer start running on the fish. Allow each coat to dry before applying the next. Three or four coats should be applied in all.

Fish should not be finished in extremely damp weather unless absolutely necessary. When the humidity is very high it sometimes causes the lacquer to "bloom," or turn milky in places. This is caused by moisture trapped in the finish coat as it is being applied. This condition can usually be corrected by spraying a little pure lacquer thinner on the affected areas with your airbrush, and then drying the area as quickly as possible near a heater or by blowing warm air on it with a hair dryer.

While these general instructions hold true for most freshwater and many saltwater fishes, there are some exceptions. Such fishes as the tarpon, sailfish, marlin, and dolphin which have rather brilliant colors and more or less basic color patterns are best treated in another way.

On these fish a better job can usually be done by spraying the whole fish with a good lacquer undercoater. Use this in your paint sprayer, not in your airbrush, and apply it quite heavily. The large-scaled fish, such as the tarpon, can be given three or four coats. Any small cracks between the scales or around the gills that still show after the undercoater has been applied should be filled with lacquer putty and then sprayed again. The fish should be absolutely free from blemishes and look like a white plaster cast before any color is applied.

Some species which have a basic silver color should next be given a coat of silver. For this, use the brightest metallic powder you can get, and mix it with lacquer thinner only. Never use ready-mixed silver paint which might not be compatible with lacquer. This mixture should also be sprayed on.

Do not touch the surface of the fish after applying the silver.

Since no binder is used in it, the silver particles are loose on the surface, and fingerprints will show up very plainly.

Apply the other color on the silver with your airbrush. When all the coloring is done, apply the clear lacquer finish as already described.

The dyes used in this work are those which are soluble in alcohol or lacquer thinner. Some colors can be purchased in powder or crystal form, and some in liquid form. Some airbrush manufacturers and art supply stores sell waterproof colors especially made for use in an airbrush. These colors are dyes dissolved in alcohol and are also compatible with lacquer. These colors are very potent, but are transparent, and are very good for coloring fish.

13

Mounting Reptiles and Amphibians

The mounting of snakes holds little appeal for most taxidermists, but it is well to know how it is done. A mounted snake never fails to attract attention even though few people care to own one.

Several complicated and unsatisfactory methods have been described for mounting snakes. It is strange that so many people have tried to make a complicated job out of one that is really not so difficult.

The procedure is somewhat similar to that for mounting fish. The snake is first posed in the desired position. If the snake is not to be mounted on a flat surface it should be posed on the object it is to be mounted on, such as a rock or a limb. A thin sheet of plastic or other material should be placed between the snake and the base so as not to soil the base with plaster when making the mold. Any part of the snake's belly which does not come in contact with the base should have a sheet of stiff cardboard or sheet metal placed in contact with the exposed undersurface.

When the snake is fixed in the desired position, make a plaster mold of the entire exposed surface. The mold can be reinforced with sisal or burlap when necessary to strengthen it.

After the mold has set up hard, the snake should be removed from the mold and skinned as soon as possible, as snakes tend to deteriorate rapidly.

Small snakes are more easily mounted on a solid body, but large specimens are best mounted on a hollow body to reduce the weight.

If the specimen is large, and you want to use a hollow body, shellac and grease the undersurface of the mold and make a mold of the undersurface before removing the snake. It is a good idea to cut a series of keys or notches in the bottom surface of the top mold before making the bottom mold. These notches should be placed every 2 or 3 inches, because the bottom mold will later be cut or broken into rather small pieces, and each piece should fit back exactly in place. You will see the importance of this later.

SKINNING SNAKES

There are two ways in which snakes may be skinned for mounting. Both methods will be described, but the first method can be used in all cases and will probably give you better results in most instances.

To skin by this method, an incision is made between the ventral plates and the first row of scales on either side of the belly. See Fig. 91. This way, the incision can be closed without showing. The incision should extend from the head to the end of tail.

Most snakes are easily skinned except for the tail, which includes all that portion from the anus on back. The skin usually separates from the body quite easily, but from the anus to the tip of the tail it must be carefully cut all the way.

When the body and tail are free, proceed with the head. If you are working on a poisonous snake, it is advisable to first squeeze out as much venom as possible and then pull the fangs to eliminate the possibility of accidentally getting nicked by a fang. Fig. 92 shows the location and structure of the venom glands and the proper way to extract the venom.

In skinning the head, be very careful when you reach the eyes

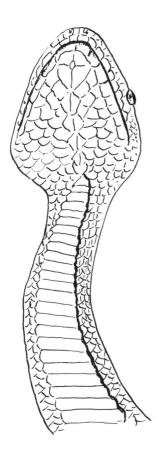

FIG. 91 When skinning a snake for mounting, make the incision between the ventral plates and the scales, as shown by the heavy line. Then you can close the incision invisibly.

not to cut the skin around them. The only other place likely to give trouble is the top of the head. The skin here grows next to the bone and must be cut and pried loose very carefully.

When you have the skin off, lay it on a smooth surface and scrape off all flesh and fat. A spoon is usually the best tool for doing this. After fleshing the skin, keep it in a 70-percent alcohol solution until you are ready to mount it.

The other method by which some snakes may be skinned is through the mouth. To do this, open the snake's mouth as wide as you can and cut the backbone where it joins the skull. Also, cut through all flesh in the neck, but do not cut through the skin. Push the backbone through the mouth and tie a strong cord around it.

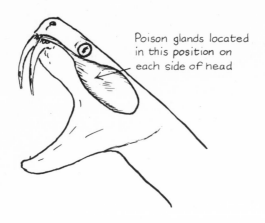

Poison glands located in this position on each side of head

To extract venom, push fangs through cloth or chamois stretched over glass and apply pressure to poison glands.

FIG. 92 A poisonous snake should have as much venom as possible extracted before skinning. Note the position of the glands. Force the fangs through a piece of cloth or chamois stretched over a glass, and press the glands on each side of the head to force out the venom.

Hang the snake up by this cord and pull the skin down over the body just as if you were pulling off a stocking.

When you reach the anus you will have to make an incision in the skin from there to the end of the tail and skin this part carefully as in the other method. The head is also skinned as in the first method.

MOUNTING SNAKES

If you are working on a small snake and are going to use a solid body, the inside of the mold should now be given a coat of shellac.

The glass eyes may be placed in the mold before the artificial body is cast. You can clearly see the imprint of the eyes in the mold. Leave a short length of wire attached to the glass eyes; put a bit of glue on each eye and set them in the proper place in the mold, letting the wire stick out into the head cavity. When using eyes with a vertical pupil, be sure that the pupil is turned the right way.

When the glue has set sufficiently, give the entire inside of the mold a coat of stearine, being careful not to dislodge the eyes.

If you are making a solid body, the mold can now be filled with plaster, hydrocal, papier mâché, or whatever you want to make the body out of. Some wires should be bent to fit in the curves of the snake and imbedded in the filling for reinforcement. Be sure that a wire goes all the way to the end of the tail. When filling the head be very careful not to displace the eyes. When the mold is full, let the body set up thoroughly before trying to remove it from the mold.

If you are going to use a hollow form, it can be made of fiberglass, laminated paper, or plaster-and-burlap. The head, however, is best made of plaster unless you are working on a very large snake such as a python, boa constrictor, or anaconda.

Build the form in the top portion of the mold first. The belly portion of the mold may then be broken or cut into short sections so you can put them in place one at a time and reach in with your fingers to build up the belly portion of the form. These pieces of the mold should be kept in order or numbered in sequence; otherwise, you will have a jigsaw puzzle to contend with.

Whether you use the solid or hollow body, the mold is carefully broken off after the body has thoroughly set or dried as the case may be. Patch any bubble holes or flaws that may be in the body,

FIG. 93 A small garter snake mounted on a solid reinforced-plaster body.

and with a sharp knife, shave a little plaster off the entire head part of the form to compensate for the thickness of the skin.

If the body is of plaster, allow it to dry thoroughly; then the entire body should be sanded down smooth, or almost so, and given at least two coats of shellac.

If the body is made of paper, plaster-and-burlap, or fiberglass, inspect it carefully for blemishes that may show through the skin, and smooth any such places. These forms, except the fiberglass, should also be given several coats of shellac.

When the form is finished you are ready to mount the skin. Remove it from the alcohol and do any additional fleshing that may be necessary. Soak the skin for a few minutes in borax water to relax it thoroughly. Dry off the excess water with paper towels, and give the inside of the skin a light coat of glycerine.

The skin is glued to the form with skin paste, Formula #1, or with any good glue that will allow you to slide the skin and does not set up too fast.

Start at the head end and paint paste on the form a few inches at a time, fitting the skin as you go. Check often to see that you are not pushing the skin too far forward or too far backward. A snake skin is very stretchy and is much longer than the body, so the objective is to make the skin and body come out even when you get to the tail. This is why it is important to use a paste that will allow you to slide the skin freely. The scales must be pushed closer together on the inside curves and not so close on the outside curves.

Fit the incision together carefully as you go. The incision does not need to be sewn except on very large snakes.

Thin strips of gauze may be wrapped in a spiral around the body to hold the skin in place until the paste sets.

Some snakes hold their color indefinitely while others fade quite rapidly, particularly the ones with bright colors such as the coral snake, rainbow snake, and emerald tree boa. The colors which fade can be restored with dyes or paints, whichever seem most suitable. The snake is finished with a coat of clear gloss lacquer or satin-finish lacquer, depending on the original texture of the skin.

If a snake has been skinned through the mouth, the skin should be coated inside with paste and slipped on the form from the tail end like pulling on a sock. More paste can be applied to the body as you go. When the skin is completely on the form, slide it around until it is in the proper position before the paste begins to set. Sew up the tail incision and finish the snake as already described.

This method sounds easier and simpler than the first method, but it is actually more difficult.

OPEN-MOUTH SNAKE MOUNTS

If you wish to mount a snake with the mouth open, you can prop the mouth open with small wires to hold it in the desired position. If it is a poisonous snake and the fangs are to be extended, they should also be held in the extended position so the gums will be in the right shape. With the mouth thus fixed, make an impression of the inside of the mouth with dental impression material, and without removing the impression, go ahead and make the mold of the snake as described earlier.

When you are ready to cast the head of the snake in making the artificial body, place the mouth impression in the mold and you will get a perfect reproduction of the inside of the mouth. If the fangs are to be extended, bore little holes in the plaster mouth and cement the fangs in place. You can clean the natural fangs and use them or make artificial ones if you prefer.

The inside of the mouth can be finished with paint, or it can be coated with a thin layer of acrylic plastic.

Instead of casting the mouth in plaster, you can make a cast of acrylic plastic in the impression material mold and then set this cast in the mold of the snake when making the body.

MOUNTING COBRAS

To mount a cobra with the hood spread, lay the front end of the snake on a piece of paper or cardboard. Spread the hood out in the proper shape, and hold it in place with pins. Draw a pattern of the hood and cut it out of sheet metal.

Make an incision between the ventral plates and the scales just large enough to insert the metal pattern under the skin in front of the neck. Pull the skin back together and make a few stitches to hold it in place. Arrange the snake in the proper pose and then make the mold as previously described. Fig. 94 shows a king cobra mounted in this manner.

FIG. 94   A king cobra with spread hood mounted on a hollow fiberglass body.

MOUNTING TURTLES

The mounting of ordinary turtles is not very difficult, but some of the larger species, which you are not likely to get anyway, can be quite a chore.

Most turtles have a hard, bony top shell called the carapace, and a bottom shell called the plastron. The top and bottom shells are held together on the sides as shown in Fig. 95.

To skin a turtle, the bottom shell is removed by sawing through the connecting shell on the sides and cutting the skin around the remainder of the body as shown by the dotted line in Fig. 95. The

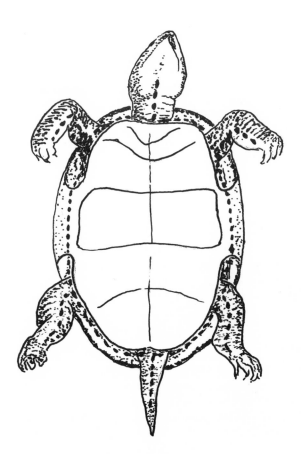

FIG. 95   When skinning a turtle, make the incisions indicated by the dotted lines. You will have to saw through the shell on each side.

incision is made near the plastron, but leave enough skin attached to the plastron to be sewn later. The legs, head, and tail are left attached to the top shell.

When the plastron, or bottom shell, has been removed, clean out all flesh from the body; skin the legs just as in skinning a small mammal. Cut the muscles from the legs and feet, but leave the bone intact. Skin the tail out to the tip and remove the bone from it. The head cannot be skinned out completely as in a bird or mammal, but you can skin down to the base of the skull and cut the neck off where it joins the head. Remove the brain and cut all flesh from the skull and mouth. The eyes may be removed from the outside or through the mouth.

When the skin and shell are clean, wash them thoroughly in water to remove all blood and fluids. Soak the skin and shell in denatured alcohol for a few minutes and then in borax water.

To start the actual mounting, a core is made of balsa wood or excelsior to fit inside the body cavity. Sharpened wires are run through the legs from the bottom of the feet, and the leg muscles are replaced by wrapping the bone and wire with tow or sisal. This wrapping should be coated with slow-setting papier mâché so the muscles and wrinkles can be modeled in the leg from the outside. The wires are anchored in the core just as in mounting a bird or small mammal. The tail and neck are also wound on wires and anchored through the core in the same manner.

Coat the sawed edge of the top and bottom shells with a good glue, such as epoxy, and bind the two shells together securely until the glue sets.

Sew the incision around the rest of the body. It may be necessary to fill in with papier mâché around the edges and at the base of the legs.

Bend the legs into the proper position as soon as possible and model them into shape. Put more papier mâché into the mouth and neck areas if needed, and model the wrinkles in the neck. Set the glass eyes in a little papier mâché.

When the skin is completely dry, any stitches that show can be modeled over with modeling wax, Formula #4.

Colors may be restored to the skin and shell with dyes or paints, depending upon the colors and the texture of the areas to be colored.

MOUNTING LIZARDS

There are so many sizes, shapes, and varieties of lizards that, obviously, no single method of mounting would suffice for all.

Some species of lizards are so small and delicate that it is impossible to skin and mount them by any conventional taxidermic method. If such specimens are to be preserved and displayed in a lifelike attitude, the freeze-dry process should be considered. This is not true taxidermy, but has been used with quite good results, even on some larger specimens.

In this process, the specimen is posed in the desired position and dehydrated in a partial vacuum at a very low temperature. Under carefully controlled conditions, the dehydration takes place without any appreciable shrinkage, and the specimen retains its natural shape indefinitely. Glass eyes may be installed and the colors restored as in a mounted specimen.

Such lizards as the horned toad may be mounted in much the same manner as a small mammal except that the incision must be made all the way from the end of the tail to the head, and the legs must usually also be split to skin them properly. Also, the head cannot be skinned and must be cleaned from the inside the same as with a turtle.

The artificial body may be made of excelsior or carved in balsa wood. The bones are left in the legs, and the legs are wired the same way as with a small mammal. More papier mâché is used in the legs, however, so they can be modeled into shape from the outside.

Most of the larger lizards are also mounted in the same way. Some, however, such as the Gila monster and Mexican beaded lizard, which have a rather firm body and large, fleshy tail, can easily be mounted on a hollow form by making a mold of the body as you do for a snake or a fish. The legs are not included in the mold. They are skinned and wired as described for a horned toad, and the wires are anchored in the artificial body.

If you lay the lizard flat on its belly when making the mold, it is not necessary to make a mold of the underside. The mold should be painted inside with a thin coat of plaster to partially compensate for the thickness of the skin. When the form is made inside, it can also be left open on the bottom until the leg wires are anchored inside. The bottom portion can then be closed by covering it with fiberglass or by filling the form with wadded paper and then modeling over it with papier mâché.

The very large lizards such as some of the giant iguanas and the dragon lizard of Komodo should be modeled in clay and mounted on a hollow manikin as described for large mammals.

The skins of most lizards can be treated with alcohol before mounting, but the large, heavy-skinned varieties should be at least partially tanned. Fig. 96 shows a common Mexican iguana which was mounted on an excelsior body.

FIG. 96   A common iguana mounted on a wrapped excelsior body which was covered with papier mâché.

MOUNTING FROGS

Frogs, like snakes, may be skinned either through the mouth or through a belly incision.

To skin a frog through the mouth, open the mouth as wide as possible and cut the backbone where it joins the skull. Also, cut the flesh and membranes around this area, but do not cut through the skin. Force the end of the backbone through the mouth, and pull the body out of the skin, turning the skin wrong side out. The body can be pulled completely out of the skin, toes and all, but if the frog is to be mounted in a sitting position, it is easier to get the correct shape if you leave the leg bones attached just as you would in a small mammal.

To do this, expose the leg all the way to the toes, but do not pull the skin all the way off the feet. Disjoint the legs where they join the body, and strip the flesh from the bone.

The skull should be left in the skin, but cut off all the flesh you can and remove the eyes and brain.

Soak the skin in alcohol until you are about ready to mount it and then put it in borax water for a few minutes before you are ready to start the actual mounting.

You will need four wires sharpened on one end for the legs and another wire to help support the head. Run a sharpened wire into the bottom of each foot and up along the leg bone. Wrap the bone and wire with tow to partially replace the muscles of the leg, but leave the wrapping a little smaller than the actual leg. Spread the wrapping with slow-setting papier mâché and pull the leg back down into the leg skin. Work more papier mâché down into the leg and force it all the way down until the leg is full.

Make a balsa-wood core just large enough so that it will barely go through the mouth into the body of the skin. Push the leg wires through this core and anchor them firmly in the balsa wood. When this is done, fill the rest of the skin with papier mâché around the balsa-wood core. Be sure to get the papier mâché in all areas of the head where you removed flesh from the skull.

Before closing the mouth, run the other wire into the balsa-wood core and bend a loop in the front end of the wire. This loop is imbedded in the papier mâché in the mouth area and will support the head until the papier mâché sets up.

Carefully bend the legs into the desired position, and shape the body as necessary before the papier mâché hardens. Take a few stitches around the mouth to hold it closed. The toes should be spread in a natural position and held in place with pins until they dry. Put a little papier mâché in the eyesockets and set the glass eyes.

When the papier mâché has hardened in the body, take a sharp needle and pierce the skin in a number of places all over the body. This will allow the papier mâché inside to dry out faster.

When the specimen is thoroughly dry, the colors may be restored with paints or dyes. When this is dry, apply a final coat of clear shellac.

If the belly incision was used in skinning, the mounting is done in the same way except that the body core can be larger; in fact, it can be carved the size and shape of the body and only a thin layer of papier mâché used between it and the skin. When the specimen is dry, the incision underneath can be modeled over with wax, Formula #4.

14

Preparing Specimens for Scientific Study

The preparation of scientific study specimens is not in the usual province of the taxidermist, but if you have the occasion to work for a museum or other scientific or educational institution, you might well be called upon to do such work.

In collecting specimens for study purposes, the collecting data is just as important as the skin. Without this information the skin is worth little or nothing.

Specimens of birds and small mammals are usually made into what are called study skins. These, along with at least part of the collection data and the skull, are kept in special drawers or cabinets in museums and other institutions for study and research purposes. It is usually desirable to have a number of specimens of the same species taken at different times of the year and in different localities in order to study color variations, etc.

When collecting specimens for scientific study, each specimen should be tagged with a label containing the following information:

1. A number assigned to the specimen by the collector.
2. Geographical location where the specimen was taken.
3. Date.
4. Sex of the specimen, indicated by ♂ for male and ♀ for female.
5. For mammals, measurement in millimeters of total length; length of tail not including hair; and length of hind foot from heel to end of longest toe, including the claw.
6. Name of collector.

All labels should be printed in black waterproof ink.

A catalog or notebook should be kept in which each specimen is numbered with the same number as the one on the tag attached to the specimen. The catalog should contain all information recorded on the tag, and any additional information that may seem worthwhile, such as notes on food habits, observations of life history, and any physical characteristics that may not be visible on the dried skin.

The sex of birds can be determined by opening the body after skinning. The sex organs will be found on either side of the backbone. See Fig. 97. The sex of small mammals can usually be determined by external examination of the genitals. Internal dissection is rarely necessary.

MAKING STUDY SKINS

Birds: The bird is skinned and treated with borax or arsenic as described in Chapter 2. (Since study skins are usually kept in dark cabinets, they are more subject to attacks by insects than mounted specimens. For this reason, arsenic is usually used instead of borax.)

Place a ball of cotton in each eyesocket, and wrap the leg bones and wingbones with cotton to replace the muscles. They need not be wired as if the bird were to be mounted.

Various methods are used by different individuals for filling the body, but one of the simplest and best methods is to wind a soft body of sisal or fine excelsior into the general shape of the natural body. This does not need to be as firm and hard as for a mounted bird. See Fig. 98.

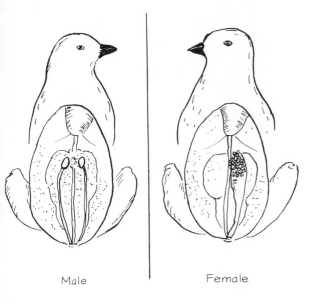

Male   Female

FIG. 97   If you are unable to determine the sex of a bird by external examination, open the body cavity. Look along the inside wall of the lower back. The kidneys are dark-colored elongated organs on each side of the backbone. In the male bird the testes will be apparent—small whitish bean-shaped organs, next to the kidneys. In the female the ovary will usually be in the same location and will usually contain many small eggs.

FIG. 98   An artificial body for a bird study skin is made much like one for a mounted bird, but it need not be packed so tightly.

A small wire may be run through the body, and the neck wound on this with cotton. When this is done, insert the body in the skin and sew up the incision. The end of the neck wire may be run through the top of the head or out the mouth and cut off inside the mouth. Stuff a little cotton into the mouth and throat area if needed to fill out the skin. Take a stitch through the beak to hold the mouth closed.

Arrange the bird in the position shown in Fig. 99. Wrap a thin sheet of cotton around the body to hold the wings and feathers in place, and allow the specimen to dry. The data tag should be attached to the legs of the bird.

FIG. 99   The correct shape for a finished bird study skin.

Small Mammals: Small mammals to be made into study skins should be skinned as described in Chapter 3. The skull should always be cleaned and numbered the same number as the skin. In mammal identification, the skull is often as important as the skin, sometimes more so.

If the skin is dirty or greasy it should be washed in soapy water or gasoline and dried with sawdust or cornmeal. The skin may be treated with borax, but a mixture of equal parts of white arsenic and alum is better. Apply this liberally to all parts of the skin inside.

Take a few stitches in the lips to hold the mouth closed. The leg bones are wrapped with cotton or tow to replace the muscles, but the legs need not be wired.

A crude body is made of sisal or excelsior the length of the natural body including the head. The body does not have to be packed as firmly as for a mounted animal, but it should be smooth and free from lumps. Run a sharpened wire through the body for the tail, and wind the tail with cotton. See Fig. 100.

Insert the body in the skin and sew up the incision, starting from the rear. Add more cotton or tow around the base of the legs if needed to fill out and smooth the skin. When the incision is sewn

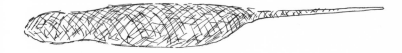

FIG. 100   An artificial body for a small mammal study skin is nothing more than a loosely wound mass of excelsior or sisal with a wire running through it for a tail. An artificial skull is not necessary.

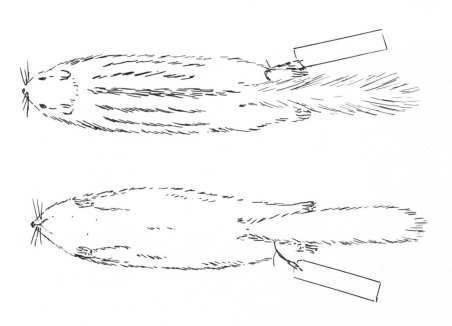

FIG. 101   Bottom and top view of a small mammal study skin.

up, shape the skin as shown in Fig. 101. Pin the feet to a board until the skin is dry. The data label should be attached to the right hind leg.

REPTILES AND AMPHIBIANS

Reptiles and amphibians are not made into study skins, but are usually pickled in a preserving solution and kept in glass jars. Either alcohol or formaldehyde may be used as a preservative. If alcohol is used, it should be at least 70 percent for small specimens, and 85 to 90 percent for larger, more fleshy specimens.

Commercial formaldehyde is usually sold in a 40-percent solution. This should be diluted before being used as a preservative. One part of 40-percent formaldehyde to 9 or 10 parts of water is the usual strength for snakes, frogs, etc. For small specimens that are not too fleshy, 1 part formaldehyde to 15 to 20 parts of water may be used. If too strong a solution is used it shrinks and hardens the specimens too much.

Specimens to be preserved should have several small slits or incisions made in the body wall so that the preservative can reach the internal organs. Large specimens should be injected in various parts of the body with the solution before being immersed. A hypodermic syringe can be used for this.

Large, fleshy specimens sometimes have enough body fluids to dilute the preservative and allow spoilage. In such cases the solution should be changed after a few days rather than using a stronger solution.

If a little borax is added to the formaldehyde it will help to preserve the colors in the specimens.

Preserving solutions, either alcohol or formaldehyde, make the specimens quite hard and stiff; therefore, the specimens should be placed in a position that will display them to the best advantage. Lizards, frogs, etc. can be pinned to a piece of cardboard or wood until they set. Snakes should be neatly coiled in the jars and not folded in all directions. The data label should be attached to the specimen, and all parts of the specimen must be covered with the preservative at all times.

15

Building Natural Habitat Groups

The building of elaborate natural habitat groups such as those found in some of our larger museums is probably a thing of the past. Some of these groups cost as much as fifty thousand dollars to build back in the days when labor and material were comparatively cheap. This, of course, included trips to far corners of the world to collect the animals and to collect material for the foreground and background scene. Some groups required many thousands of leaves, each of which were cast in wax and hand-colored. To duplicate such groups today in the same manner, a museum would have to have an enormous budget.

This is not the type of project we are concerned with here. The kind of natural habitat group to be discussed in this chapter is the small, more or less portable group which can be built in your shop at a reasonable cost. These groups make beautiful displays, and can sometimes be sold to schools, businesses, or private individuals for use in homes. These displays can be made as elaborate as your time and talent permit, but there are certain basic rules you should follow to get the best results from your efforts.

If you have talent for painting landscapes, your possibilities are almost unlimited. Otherwise, your groups must be strictly a "one-spot" scene without much depth.

In small groups you can use small mounted animals, or you can make models of large animals and construct the foreground and background in proportion.

Ordinarily, natural habitat groups are constructed with a curved background so there are no corners to distract attention from the exhibit. In this way you can also achieve a greater illusion of depth.

For best results, the distance from the front to the back of the case should be approximately 60 percent of the width across the front. For example, if the case is 3 feet wide in front, it should be approximately 22 inches deep from front to back; and if it is 4 feet wide, it should be about 29 inches deep. The glass in front should be smaller than the front of the case so that the background will be approximately the same distance from the eyes of the viewer on both the sides and the back. See Fig. 102.

To cut a pattern, first decide on the width and depth of the case and cut a rectangular sheet of paper to those proportions. Fold the paper end to end so the corners are exactly even. Draw a nice, even curve around one corner and cut along this line. When you spread the paper back out you will have your pattern for the top and bottom of the case.

Cut two pieces of three-quarter-inch plywood the size of your pattern. Measure the distance around the curve of the plywood from front corner to front corner, and get a piece of galvanized sheet metal this length. The width of sheet metal to buy will depend upon how high you want the case to be from top to bottom. Usually 3 feet is enough height for a group that is 3 or 4 feet wide, but sometimes 4 feet is better, as you will see later.

Use small galvanized shingle nails and nail one edge of the sheet metal around the curve of one piece of your plywood. When this is done, nail the other edge to the other piece of plywood in the same manner. See Fig. 103. After the sheet metal is nailed to both pieces of the plywood, a piece of 2x2-inch lumber should be put in each front corner. Nails are driven through both the top and bottom plywood into the ends of the 2x2s, and the sheet metal is also nailed to them on the sides. This will make the case rigid and keep the sides straight up and down.

A light fixture, preferably fluorescent, should be installed along

FIG. 102   The front panel of a small natural habitat group. Making the front window smaller than the front of the case permits the viewer to see the sides and back of the background scene from approximately the same distance. The glass is set in at the bottom to help eliminate distracting reflections.

FIG. 103   Top and bottom of a small natural habitat group case with sheet metal in place around the curve.

the top front of the case where it will not be visible when the front of the case is installed.

The sheet metal inside the case should now be washed with vinegar or a weak solution of acetic acid. This will slightly eat into the galvanized surface and make the paint adhere much better.

After the surface is thoroughly dry it is given a coat of unthinned white lead and then stippled with a stippling brush. The white lead is quite thick and cannot be painted on smoothly. Just smear it as evenly as possible and finish it with the stippling brush.

If you are unable to get white lead from your paint dealer, you can use a good grade of flat white wall paint and thicken it with whiting enough so that it will hold a stippled finish.

After the base coat is dry, which will take several days if you use white lead, it may be sanded lightly to remove any high points. The stippled surface makes a good base, somewhat similar to canvas, and will take oil colors much better than a smooth surface.

Your foreground and background should be planned carefully and made to tie in with each other as closely as possible. The foreground can be built directly on the floor of the case, but it is better to cut out another piece of thinner plywood to fit the floor of the case and build the foreground on it. This will allow you to take the groundwork out of the case to work on it and will also make it easier to work on the background.

The ground can be simulated by modeling papier mâché over a burlap or wire-net base and coloring it the proper color. Real earth or sand can also be sprinkled over the papier mâché and pressed in lightly to give a more realistic texture. Some suitable artificial plants and flowers may be used, and dead natural grasses that have been soaked in a weak formaldehyde solution for a day or two and then dried can be sprayed the desired color.

Artificial rocks are made by covering a rough framework with screen wire or burlap and then modeling over it with papier mâché. It can then be colored as desired.

Unless you can draw and paint a scene freehand on the background, you will need to enlarge a series of photographs or other pictures made in panorama form. For example, if you have a panorama of three 8 x 10 photographs and your background measures 70 inches around the curve, you will need to enlarge the pictures $2\frac{1}{3}$ times to fill up the length of the background. The easiest way to do this is to make horizontal and vertical lines on the photographs 1 inch apart. Also, make horizontal and vertical lines on the background $2\frac{1}{3}$ inches apart. You can then draw the picture on the background, using the squares as a guide. When doing this it is helpful to number at least part of the squares on both the photographs and the background with corresponding numbers so you will not get lost so easily. The above figures are only an example and will not necessarily be correct in every case. If you are making a group with miniature models of large animals, the background would, of course, be painted on a different scale than if you are using small mounted animals. In other words, the background should be painted in direct proportion to the animals in the foreground.

When taking photographs or making sketches of an actual scene to be reproduced as a background scene, it is well to remember your purpose. If the foreground of your photographs or sketches starts 40 to 50 feet out in front of you, it will not tie in properly with the foreground in your group. The foreground in your pictures should start close up so as to show detail of the immediate foreground. It is usually helpful to take a few extra pictures with the camera focused up close.

If you want your background scene to represent a downhill view, such as looking down the side of a mountain into a valley, a greater illusion of depth can be achieved by using wider sheet metal for the background and building the foreground on a downhill slant from front to back. See Fig. 104.

The front of the case can be made of plywood and finished in any way you desire. The glass window in front, however, should usually be made to slant away from the viewer 2 or 3 inches at the bottom. This will keep the glass from picking up so many reflections from windows or room lights.

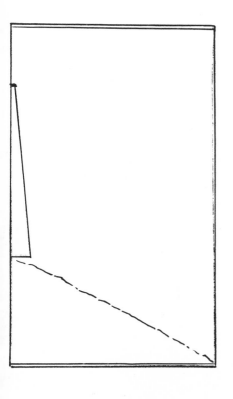

FIG. 104   Side view of natural habitat group showing how window and foreground should be arranged if scene is to be looking downhill.

MAKING AN UNDERWATER SCENE

Another type of natural habitat group that will appeal to lovers of marine life is the underwater scene. This represents a lake or other body of water above and below the surface.

In this type of group a curved background is not ordinarily used, although it could be used above the simulated water level. It can be built in a square, boxlike structure of almost any size, but will look better if it is at least 30 inches deep from front to back. Fig. 105 shows the construction. The numbers below correspond with the numbers on the diagram.

1. Back of case. This should be painted white.
2. Fluorescent light.
3. Vertical glass about 3 inches from white background. This glass is sprayed with blue to represent the sky above the horizontal glass #7. A few blotches may be rubbed out of the blue to let the white background show through to represent clouds. The landscape on the opposite shoreline can also be painted on this glass. Below the waterline you can leave the glass clear or paint some underwater plants, rocks, etc. on it.
4. Another vertical glass about 3 inches from glass #3. This glass may be omitted, but will give a greater illusion of distance if you paint something on it which would appear out in the water such as a rock jetty, an island, a pier, or a boat. Under the surface it may also have something painted on it that would be under the water.
5. This is still another vertical glass about 2 or 3 inches behind the front glass. This glass extends only from the bottom up to the horizontal glass which represents the surface of the water. This, or any of the glasses, may be stippled lightly with varnish or clear lacquer on the back side to give a slightly dimmer effect.
6. This is the front viewing window.
7. Horizontal glass to represent surface of water.

The bottom of the case may be covered with papier mâché, sand, or artificial rocks to represent the kind of bottom you want. It should be sprayed or painted with varnish to make it look wet. Artificial underwater plants can be used on the bottom, or can be painted on the glasses, or both.

Small mounted fish or other marine life may be attached to the glasses with epoxy glue or placed on the bottom.

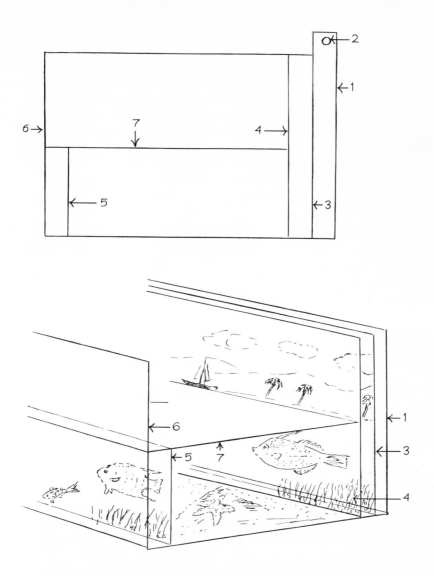

FIG. 105   End view of underwater scene showing placement of the various pieces of glass. The numbers are explained in the text.

As a variation of this exhibit, you can omit the horizontal glass and the painting on glasses #3 and #4 and let glass #5 extend all the way to the top. This will make the whole scene appear as under water.

FIG. 106 The American Museum of Natural History in New York City has extraordinary bioramas on display. These whitetail deer are mounted in an environment as authentic and natural as the museum's staff of scientists and artists could produce.

FIG. 107 At the Museum of Natural History, even the humble jackrabbit becomes the centerpiece of a fascinating slice of nature. The museum's bioramas may be the high point of the art of taxidermy, but a careful home taxidermist can achieve good results too.

Appendix:
Tools, Materials, and Formulas

There are many tools that can be used in taxidermy, but only a few that are indispensable. In the beginning it would not be wise to invest heavily in tools and supplies. With proper tools the work is, of course, made easier and more enjoyable, but some of the best work has been done with the simplest equipment.

Much of the equipment needed to start doing taxidermy can usually be found around the home. Below is a list of tools and supplies that will be needed to mount birds and small mammals. Other tools and products are mentioned in the text from time to time. These may be acquired as needed.

Small knife or scalpel for skinning
Sharpening stone
Pliers
Drill and assortment of bits
Hammer
Saw
Tape measure
Artist's brushes

Assortment of oil colors and turpentine for thinning
Tweezers (preferably long and pointed)
Galvanized wire (assorted sizes)
Needles (three-cornered hide needles and curved surgeon's needles are best)
Sewing thread (button and carpet thread)
Straight pins
Cotton
Excelsior
String (ordinary grocer's twine)
Papier mâché or water putty
Powdered borax
Plaster of Paris (preferably molding plaster)
Assortment of glass eyes

The above list is quite basic and consists of items that should be on hand at all times.

Following is a list, in alphabetical order, of all tools, materials, and supplies that are mentioned in the text, with explanatory or instructional notes pertinent to their use in taxidermy:

Acetic acid   A colorless, pungent, mobile liquid. Vinegar is a weak form of acetic acid. It is sometimes used in tanning processes, and also to cut into galvanized surfaces to make paint adhere better.

Acetone   A highly inflammable liquid solvent. It is used to clean brushes used in fiberglass resin before the plastic sets up. It is also used to dissolve fats and cellulose products.

Acrylic paint   A paint that is similar to oil colors in texture, but is soluble in water, and dries much faster than oil colors.

Acrylic plastic   A plastic resin made in powder form in various colors. When combined with a liquid catalyst, it sets up into a hard, durable plastic. It is used by dental technicians for making dental plates, and can also be used in taxidermy for making artificial teeth and mouth parts.

Airbrush   This is really not a brush, but a small adjustable spraygun. It is usually about the size of a fountain pen. In fish taxidermy it is almost indispensable for applying color to a mounted fish. Many other uses will also be found for it in the taxidermy shop.

Air compressor   As the name implies, this is a machine capable of compressing air and releasing it at a steady rate. When used in connection with an airbrush, a pressure regulator may be needed to adjust the pressure to suit the particular airbrush you are using.

Arsenic Sodium arsenite, a deadly poison. Arsenic was formerly used extensively in taxidermy to poison skins before mounting. It is unequaled as a protection against bugs, and is still used a great deal, but most taxidermists now use powdered borax instead. If used at all, arsenic should be used with extreme caution. A very small amount can be deadly if taken internally, and it is extremely irritating to tender or broken skin.

Alum A common name applied to any of a series of double crystalline salts. Ammonium and potash alum are perhaps the most common forms, and either may be used whenever alum is called for in the text.

Aluminum foil Thin sheet aluminum, sold in convenient rolls. Since it is a positive moisture barrier and will conform to almost any surface, it is ideal for wrapping small specimens to be frozen. It can also be used as a separator when using fiberglass over plaster.

Aluminum sulfate This is another form of alum often used in the tanning business. It has certain advantages over the other forms of alum in that it does not shrink skins quite as much, and tends to give them more stretch.

Aniline dye Aniline is a colorless, oily liquid which is the base of many coal-tar dyes. These dyes are very potent, and can be thinned with alcohol or lacquer thinner for use in taxidermy work.

Artist's brush Small, long-handled artist's brushes are made in a variety of shapes and sizes. They are useful in doing fine detail work such as painting thin eyelids.

Asbestos A noninflammable magnesium silicate mineral which is fibrous in structure. Finely ground asbestos can be used in addition to, or in place of, paper pulp in making papier mâché.

Awl A small sharp-pointed tool which is similar to an icepick but usually shorter.

Baking soda Sodium bicarbonate, a common alkali, often used in taxidermy to neutralize acids.

Balsa wood A very soft, lightweight wood which grows in tropical America. Because of its soft texture it can be easily carved and is, therefore, useful for making artificial skulls and whole bodies for birds and small mammals. In thin sheets it is ideal for carding the fins of mounted fish.

Beeswax   Natural beeswax is ideal for waxing sewing thread to increase its strength. White, or bleached, beeswax is often used in combination with other waxes, and other ingredients, to make a better casting or modeling wax. White beeswax is best for this since it can be more easily colored to the desired shade than natural wax.

Bone knife   A knife with a rather long blade which is designed for disjointing bones in hard-to-reach places.

Borax   A white crystalline compound which is often used in taxidermy as a cleaning agent, and to discourage insects which often attack skins.

Boric acid   A white crystalline mildly acidic compound. In solution, it is a mild antiseptic. It is often used in taxidermy to neutralize the lime in dehairing solutions.

Brain spoon   A small tool with a spoon-shaped end which is designed for removing the brain of birds and small mammals. A small wire bent into the shape of a hairpin usually works better.

Calipers   A tool with two curved arms which are hinged together on one end. Calipers are useful for measuring the distance between two points which cannot be measured with a straight measuring device.

Carbolic acid   Phenol, a crystalline solid which melts at 41° C. and boils at 182° C. It is corrosive and poisonous, but in a dilute form is used as an antiseptic and disinfectant. It is sometimes used in taxidermy to prevent or retard spoilage in skins.

Catalyst   The name given to any agent which either speeds up or retards a chemical reaction. In working with plastics, a catalyst is generally used to make the plastic resin set up.

C-clamp   As the name implies, a clamp shaped like the letter C with a screw adjustment. These clamps are made in a variety of sizes. A variety of them will be found useful in any shop.

Chloroform   A volatile colorless liquid. It is sometimes used in medicine as a general or local anesthetic. Prolonged breathing causes death; therefore it can be used to kill specimens painlessly and without damage to the skin.

Cornmeal   A meal made by grinding corn. It is highly absorbent, and is useful in taxidermy to absorb body fluids when skinning specimens. It can also be used with gasoline for cleaning fur.

Cotton   The cotton used in taxidermy should be clean, long-fibered, and free from lumps.

Currier's knife   A specialized tool with removable blades which have a sharp, turned edge. It is useful for shaving down hides before tanning.

Denatured alcohol   One of many types of alcohol. Denatured alcohol is excellent for thinning shellac, for pickling small mammal skins, for preserving biological specimens, and as a solvent for certain dyes. It is useful to have on hand at all times.

Dental impression material   Several forms of dental impression material are sold, such as gum, paste, and powder. It is useful for making quick, temporary molds or impressions. In taxidermy the powdered form is usually most suitable.

Dextrine   Commercial dextrine, also known as British gum, is a colorless or yellowish powder resembling starch in composition. When mixed with water it forms a strong adhesive, and has many uses in taxidermy work.

Diagonal cutters   A tool similar to pliers except that both jaws have a cutting rather than a holding edge. This tool is handy for cutting both wire and small bones. It is particularly useful when skinning small fish.

Drill   A tool for boring holes. Some type of drill is needed in every taxidermy shop. The beginner can usually get by with a simple twist drill or a bit brace. An electric drill is, of course, much faster and easier to use.

Ear opener   A tool similar to long-nosed pliers except that when the handles are squeezed, the jaws open instead of close. Ear openers are very helpful when skinning the ears of large mammals.

Emery wheel   An abrasive wheel which is turned either by a motor or a hand crank. It is useful for sharpening wires and some tools.

Epoxy glue   A plastic glue which requires a catalyst to make it set up. It is useful when a super-strong, permanent bond is required.

Essence of pearl   This is finely ground mother-of-pearl in a lacquer base. It is usually sold in either a liquid or a paste form, and can be thinned with lacquer thinner to the desired consistency. It can be applied with a brush, but far better results are usually obtained by spraying. Essence of pearl is almost essential in obtaining an iridescent effect on mounted fish.

Ether   A colorless, highly volatile and inflammable liquid which is used as an anesthetic in medicine, and commercially as a solvent for fats and oils. Like chloroform, prolonged breathing of ether will cause death; therefore, it can be used to kill specimens.

Excelsior   Excelsior is nothing more than finely shredded wood. For taxidermy use, that made from basswood, or other soft wood, is best.

Fiberglass resin   A plastic resin sold in liquid form. When combined with a catalyst, it sets up to form a hard, rather brittle solid. When reinforced with glass cloth or glass mat, it is very tough and durable.

File   Files are made in many sizes and shapes for different purposes. A small assortment is useful in any shop.

Formaldehyde   Formaldehyde, or formalin, is sold commercially in a 40-percent solution. It is a gaseous compound of carbon, hydrogen, and oxygen. It has a strong, suffocating odor. It is useful in preserving biological specimens.

Galvanized wire   Iron wire which has been treated with a zinc or tin coating, thereby preventing rust. Any wire subject to rust or corrosion should be avoided in taxidermy for use inside specimens.

Gambier   An earthy-looking substance produced from the leaves of a Malayan shrub. It is used extensively in the tanning and dyeing industries.

Gasoline   Whenever gasoline is called for in taxidermy, white gasoline is preferable, since it does not contain lead or other additives.

Glass cloth   A cloth made from spun glass fibers. When incorporated with polyester or epoxy resin, it reinforces, and imparts tremendous strength to the finished product.

Glycerine   A colorless, odorless liquid with a sweet taste. Its chief source is as a by-product in the manufacture of soap, but it has many uses in industry. In taxidermy, it can be used in place of oil in tanning. It can also be used on bird, fish, and other animal skins to retard drying and to prevent cracking.

Hammer   Several types of hammers are made for various specific uses. Every taxidermy shop should be equipped with an ordinary claw hammer and a small tack hammer.

Hook and chain   Hook and chain sets are sold by taxidermy supply houses for hanging birds and small mammals while skinning. A similar set can be homemade by filing the barbs off fish hooks of the proper size and attaching small chains or wires through the eyes of the hooks.

Hydrated lime   Hydrated, or slaked, lime, calcium hydroxide, is the most common form in which lime is sold. It is used in taxidermy for removing the hair from skins to be made into buckskin or leather.

Hydrocal The commercial name for a form of gypsum plaster. It has about the same setting speed as molding plaster, but it gets much harder.

Hypodermic syringe A glass or metal tube which is fitted with a hollow needle on one end and a plunger on the other. It is designed to inject fluids through, or into, flesh. In preparing biological specimens, it is used to inject alcohol or formaldehyde into the tissues, or into the body cavity of the specimen.

Kerosene A petroleum product which is more oily, and less inflammable, than gasoline. Its main use in taxidermy is in preparing stearine to be used as a separator in molds. See Formula #8.

Knife Many sizes, shapes, and qualities of knives are on the market. The choice of knives for taxidermy varies with each individual and the type of work being done. A knife of good-quality steel is essential when much skinning is to be done.

Lacquer Lacquer is a mixture of either natural or synthetic resins dissolved in a volatile organic solvent. Quick-drying synthetic lacquer is usually made from a cellulose base. As compared to oil paints, lacquer has the advantage of drying in a very few minutes; oil paints require several hours, or even days in some cases. Oil-base paints can be applied over a lacquer surface, but lacquer cannot be applied over an oil-paint surface. Some lacquers can be applied with a brush, but best results are usually obtained by spraying.

Lacquer thinner A highly volatile, inflammable solvent. It is useful not only for thinning lacquer, but also for cleaning brushes which have been used in other paints.

Linseed oil Linseed oil is made from the seed of flax. It is useful for thinning oil-base paints; or when thinned with turpentine, for improving the appearance of antlers. See Formula #11.

Liquid latex A mixture of synthetic rubber, ammonia, and distilled water. When exposed to the air, it dries into a tough rubber. It is useful in making flexible molds.

Neat's-foot oil An animal oil used to soften and condition leather. Sulphonated oil is best for use in tanning.

Needles Ordinary sewing needles can be used for bird and small mammal work, but three-cornered hide needles and curved surgeon's needles are almost a necessity when sewing heavier hides.

Oil colors   The oil colors used in art work are made of various color pigments which are ground in oil. Some colors are transparent, others are opaque. These colors are sold in tubes, and are useful in restoring color to the fleshy parts of birds and mammals. The disadvantage in using oil colors is that they are very slow-drying. If the time factor is important, other types of colors should be used.

Papier mâché   Basically, papier mâché is a mixture of paper pulp, glue, and usually a little plaster. It can be modeled, cast in molds, or used as a surface coating. It dries into a light, fairly tough material that can be shellacked, painted, or given various other finishes. It is generally more useful in making artificial rocks and other accessories than in the actual mounting of specimens. Many taxidermists would feel helpless without it, while others use it rarely if at all.

Paraffin wax   A mineral wax which is very inert chemically. It is unaffected by most acids and alkalies, and is obtainable in various degrees of hardness. It is sometimes used alone, or in combination with other waxes, to make wax casts of certain objects.

Petroleum jelly   A clear mineral grease which can be used to grease the shellacked surface of plaster molds to prevent casts from sticking. Stearine is generally better for this, however.

Pinking machine   A small machine with a hand crank which turns a cutting wheel. It cuts a small scallop with a pinked edge, and is used to cut felt borders for rugs. It can also be used to cut strips of buckskin for decorative use when mounting antlers on a wall panel.

Pliers   Many sizes and shapes of pliers are on the market. At least one good pair should be in every shop.

Plaster of Paris   Several types of plaster are available. It all looks about the same, but each type has a different setting speed, and some types get harder than others. All types of plaster are likely to vary somewhat from one batch to the next, depending upon the age of the plaster, the amount of exposure it has had to the air, and the temperature of the water it is mixed with. Under normal conditions, the differences are about as follows:

Dental plaster   is the fastest setting. It will usually harden in five to ten minutes, which is too fast for most taxidermy jobs.

Casting plaster   will usually set up in about fifteen minutes. It is good for making casts or for making small molds which can be made quickly. It is still too fast for many jobs in taxidermy, especially if the operator is not skilled in plaster work.

Molding plaster   will harden in approximately thirty minutes. This is about right for making most molds. It usually gives you plenty of time to apply the plaster before it starts to set up.

Gauging plaster   is very slow. It is used mostly for plastering walls, and generally takes several hours to harden.

It is helpful to know the approximate setting time of your plaster before starting a job. The setting time can be altered somewhat by the addition of certain additives to the water before mixing the plaster. A small amount of salt added to the water will hasten the setting time, but slightly weakens the plaster. Alum also speeds the setting time, and without weakening the plaster. Dextrine solution added to the water will make the plaster harder and tougher, but in time it tends to disintegrate and make the plaster become chalky. Vinegar retards the setting time without affecting the hardness. Borax also retards the setting time, and makes the plaster much harder.

Mixing instructions: The correct mixing of plaster is important if good results are to be achieved. Either a plastic bowl or a glazed pottery bowl makes the best container for mixing. The hardened leftover plaster can easily be removed from these containers without damaging the container. With a little experience, you can anticipate the approximate amount of mix that will be needed. Put about one-third that much water in the container and then sift the plaster, rather slowly, into the water. Continue this until the plaster makes a little mound, or island, above the water. If you want a rather thin mix, it should then be about right. If you want a thicker mix, add a little more plaster. In either case, do not stir the mixture until all the plaster has absorbed water and becomes visibly damp; otherwise, the plaster will be lumpy. When all the plaster has become damp, stir with a spoon, or with your fingers, until the mixture is smooth and creamy. You can tap the bottom of the bowl on a hard surface to make any air bubbles come to the top. The mixture is then ready to use.

Plastic wood   Plastic wood can be bought in cans or tubes, and is ideal for small repair jobs such as filling cracks in lips and eyelids. It dries in a short time, and can be sanded perfectly smooth.

Polyester resin   See **Fiberglass resin.**

Potassium permanganate   A compound of potassium, manganese, and oxygen. It is a strong oxidizing agent and is sold in crystal form. When dissolved in water, it is used in taxidermy to stain faded or bleached antlers.

Pumice stone   A volcanic glass formed by the solidification of lava permeated with gas bubbles. In powder form it is used as a polishing agent.

Rasp   A very coarse file used on wood or other materials.

Rosin   A solid residue obtained from crude turpentine. In taxidermy it is sometimes mixed with beeswax or other waxes to make a more durable wax compound. See Formula #4.

Salt   Sodium chloride. Common salt is packaged in various degrees of coarseness. For dissolving in solutions, the finer grades are best. For salting the hides of animals, the fine-grain salt is also best, since it penetrates the skin faster than the coarser grades. Feed and grain stores usually sell haying salt, or mixing salt, which is only slightly coarser than table salt but much cheaper.

Saw   Several types of saws will be found useful in the taxidermy shop. An ordinary hand saw is a must, as it can be used for sawing wood, and also for sawing off the skull plate of horned or antlered animals. A hacksaw will also be needed for cutting metal from time to time. A coping or keyhole saw will also be useful for cutting out backboards for head forms and other circular cuts. An electric saber saw is one of the best investments that can be made. It uses a variety of interchangeable blades and will, to a large extent, replace most of the other saws mentioned above, and do the job much more quickly and easily.

Scalpel   A small surgical knife with a long handle and a short blade. It is preferred by some for skinning birds and small animals.

Scissors   At least one pair of good strong scissors will be needed in every shop.

Sharpening stone   A sharpening stone or some other type of knife sharpener is necessary in any taxidermy shop.

Shellac   Shellac is made from the resinous secretion of certain Asiatic insects. This gummy substance, called lac, is dissolved in alcohol to make shellac. It is widely used as a finish on wood and to fill the pores in plaster. It is also used as a base for other finishes.

Side-cutting pliers   Pliers with a cutting edge on one side of the jaws. They are useful for cutting wire and for holding more or less flat objects. They can also be used for skin pullers at times.

Sisal   A fibrous material made from the leaves of the sisal hemp plant. It resembles excelsior but is much finer and softer. Sisal is much used in taxidermy for small artificial bodies and for reinforcement in plaster.

Skin pullers A tool similar to pliers, but with a broader head which is designed for gripping leather. Skin pullers are especially useful in mounting large mammals.

Sodium silicate This is commonly known as liquid water glass. It is sometimes used by farmers as an egg preserver. It is also used in the manufacture of glass and ceramics. In taxidermy it is sometimes used to give added hardness to laminated-paper manikins.

Stearine A mixture of stearic acid and kerosene. It is used as a separator in molds. See Formula #8.

Straight pins Common straight pins are useful in taxidermy for holding the skin down in the depressions on mounted animals until the paste underneath sets up. The larger pins, which are called banker's pins or nailing pins, are best for this.

Sulfuric acid A compound of hydrogen, sulfur, and oxygen. It is an extremely strong and corrosive acid which has many uses commercially. In taxidermy it is often used in pickling and tanning solutions. In this work the commercial sulfuric acid should be used as it is much cheaper than chemically pure acid. In any case, it should be used with extreme caution. It will cause severe burns to your skin, and will also eat holes in many types of fabric.

Tanning oil An oil used to soften and condition leather during the tanning process. Sulphonated neat's-foot oil is one of the best oils for this purpose. Butter is also sometimes used. In place of tanning oil, soap or glycerine can also be used with good results.

Tape measure A steel tape at least 6 feet in length should be standard equipment of every taxidermist.

Terra japonica "Japanese earth," a vegetable produce obtained from a Japanese plant. It is often used in tanning solutions.

Tow A soft, hairlike jute fiber which is used in bird and small-mammal taxidermy for winding necks, tails, legs, etc. Cotton can usually be used instead.

Turpentine Turpentine is made from the sap of various conifers. It is widely used as a thinner and drying agent in oil-base paints and varnishes.

Tweezers Tweezers, or forceps, are made in many shapes and sizes. They are useful for picking up and holding small objects. In taxidermy, the sharp-pointed type is especially helpful when setting glass eyes in mounted specimens.

Twine   Ordinary three- or four-ply grocer's twine is good for winding excelsior bodies for most birds and small mammals. Sometimes a lighter string is better when working on very small specimens.

Washing soda   Washing soda, or sal soda, is a form of sodium carbonate. It is used as a water softener and as a cleaning agent.

Water clay   Water clay is a natural earth clay which is plastic when wet and becomes hard when dry. Good water clay should be free from grit and other foreign matter. When mixed to the proper working consistency, it is unequaled for modeling forms, especially large forms. It can be manipulated much faster than the manufactured permanent-type modeling compositions. In some localities, excellent water clay can be found in natural deposits. It can also be bought in almost any art-supply store either in dry powdered form or ready-mixed.

Water putty   Water putty is a commercial product sold at paint and hardware stores. It is in powdered form and, like plaster, can be mixed with water as needed. Under normal conditions it sets up in about thirty minutes, and can be sanded or carved to a very smooth surface. It is very similar to the modeling composition given in Formula #6. Either of these is good for modeling the mouths of mounted fish, filling the ear butts of head mounts, and setting glass eyes.

White lead   A heavy white poisonous mixture of lead carbonate and hydrated lead oxide. It was formerly used as a base for most paints. It is slow-drying, but makes a good undercoat for other paints, except lacquer.

Whiting   Whiting is a pure form of calcium carbonate. It is a white, powdery substance which is prepared by grinding chalk, mixing it with water, and separating the fine particles. It is used commercially as a filler in paint, in making putty, and as a metal polish. In taxidermy, it is used mainly as a filler in making skin paste and modeling compositions. See Formulas #1 and #6.

FORMULAS

Formula #1: skin paste   For pasting mammal skins to manikins.
Mix equal parts, by measure, of dry dextrine and water. Heat, while stirring constantly, until all the dextrine has dissolved. Remove from heat, and stir in whiting until a thick, creamy paste is formed. To each gallon of this mixture add 1 teaspoonful of carbolic acid or 4 teaspoon-

fuls of denatured alcohol and mix thoroughly. Keep stored in a covered non-metal container.

Formula #2: borax water   For keeping skins moist and flexible while mounting.
Dissolve 4 ounces of borax in 1 gallon of water. More borax will do no harm, but 4 ounces is all that will dissolve.

Formula #3: casting wax   For casting combs, wattles, etc.
Melt together equal parts of white beeswax and paraffin wax. While still in a liquid state, color to the desired shade with oil colors dissolved in a minimum of turpentine.

Formula #4: modeling wax   For modeling around eyes, lips, etc., of mounted animals.
Melt 3 ounces of white beeswax and 1 ounce of rosin in separate containers. Color the melted beeswax to the desired shade with oil colors dissolved in a minimum of turpentine; then add the rosin. Pour into small molds to harden.

Formula #5: dextrine solution   For making skin paste as in Formula #1 above; for making papier mâché as in Formula #12-A, and for making fish mix, Formula #13.
Mix equal parts, by measure, of dry dextrine and water. Heat, while stirring, until all the dextrine has dissolved. Add 1 teaspoonful of carbolic acid or 4 teaspoonfuls of denatured alcohol to retard fermentation. Keep stored in a covered non-metal container.

Formula #6: modeling composition   Use for modeling ear butts, filling in under eyelids, lips, nostrils, etc. This becomes rock-hard in about thirty minutes.
Use skin paste, Formula #1, or dextrine solution, Formula #5, and add whiting until a very thick, gummy paste is formed. Add dry molding plaster and work it in until the composition is the consistency of thick dough or putty.

Formula #7: pickle baths   Any of the following pickle baths can be used to treat small mammal skins before mounting. They may also be used on larger skins, but far better results will be achieved if the larger skins are completely tanned before mounting.
Alum pickle: Dissolve 1 pound of salt and 1 pound of alum in 2 gallons of water. Leave the skin in this solution for several days, until it is thoroughly pickled. When ready to mount, wash the skin in plain water. Squeeze out excess water and work a little tanning oil into the flesh side of the skin. The oil should be thinned somewhat with warm

water before applying. Dry and fluff the fur by working the skin in dry borax.

Acid pickle: Dissolve 1 pound of salt in 2 gallons of warm water. Slowly add 3 ounces, by volume, of sulfuric acid while stirring constantly. Mix and keep this solution in a wood, glass, or crockery container. Place skin in the solution until thoroughly pickled. Before mounting, wash the skin thoroughly in a little water to which a handful of baking soda has been added. This will neutralize the acid. Follow with a thorough washing in plain water. Treat the skin with tanning oil as described above, before mounting.

Aluminum sulfate pickle: In 2 gallons of hot water, dissolve 5 pounds of salt, 1½ pounds of aluminum sulfate, and 4 ounces of borax. Allow the solution to cool before putting in the skin. After the skin is pickled, wash thoroughly and treat with tanning oil before mounting.

Denatured alcohol pickle: Ordinary denatured alcohol can be used in place of any of the above pickles for small skins. Use the alcohol full-strength. Small skins, such as squirrels, will usually be thoroughly pickled in one day. Wash the skin and treat with tanning oil as described in the other methods before mounting.

Formula #8: stearine   Use as a separator in molds to keep casts from sticking to the mold.

Put 12 ounces of stearic acid and 1 pint of kerosene in the top of a double boiler. Heat over boiling water until the stearic acid has melted and the mixture becomes clear. Pour into a glass jar or can to cool.

Formula #9: form paste   Use for making laminated-paper manikins.

Mix 1 cup of dry dextrine and 1 cup of rye flour together. Add enough warm water to make a creamy batter. Add this mixture to 1 gallon of boiling water. Let it boil for a few minutes while stirring constantly. When cool, this makes a paste of creamy consistency. If you like a thinner paste it can be thinned with water. If you like a thicker paste it can be thickened with dextrine solution, Formula #5. Some people also add molasses to the above mixture. This makes a tougher paste that is slightly more adhesive.

Formula #10: antler stain   Use to restore a natural color to bleached, or faded, antlers.

Dissolve ½ teaspoonful of potassium permanganate crystals in ½ cup of warm water. Apply this to the antlers with a brush or wad of cloth until the desired color is attained. This liquid is a deep purple color, but dries to a rich brown, closely simulating the natural color of antlers.

Formula #11: antler brightener   Use to brighten and improve the appearance of antlers that are dull and lifeless-looking.

Mix 3 parts of turpentine and 1 part of linseed oil. Apply this to the antlers with a brush or cloth and rub off with a dry cloth.

Formula #12-A: papier mâché   A quickly made mâché. Use for setting glass eyes, modeling over skull plates, filling ear butts, etc.

Make a thick, mushy mixture of paper pulp or ground asbestos and dextrine solution, Formula #5. Stir dry molding plaster into this mixture until it is thick enough to handle without being too sticky. If you want a lighter-weight product, with less strength, you can add vermiculite to the mixture.

Formula #12-B: old-fashioned papier mâché   Use for making artificial rocks, bark, groundwork in natural habitat groups or any job which calls for papier mâché.

Many formulas have been used for making papier mâché, but the basic ingredient in all is paper pulp. You can use finely ground asbestos instead of paper pulp, but if you want to make your own pulp it can be done as follows:

Use a can with rather high sides and fill it about ⅓ full of water. Fill the can the rest of the way with shredded newspaper or other soft paper. Never use hard-finish or glossy paper.

Put the can on the stove and bring it to a boil. Let it boil briskly for a few minutes until the paper becomes damp and begins to collapse. Remove from the stove and begin to punch and churn the paper with a blunt, rough-ended stick until it is completely broken down and becomes a smooth mass of pulp that is free from lumps. If you sprinkle a small amount of dextrine on the pulp at this time, and stir it in, it will help to soften and smooth out the pulp. Use only a very small amount of dextrine at this time, however.

When the pulp is smooth and free from lumps it can be spread out on a smooth surface and allowed to dry. When thoroughly dry, it can be crumbled up and stored for future use or mixed with other dry ingredients and used at any time by simply adding water.

The hardening time of any papier mâché is determined by the amount of plaster it contains. The toughest mâché is made of only paper pulp and glue, with little or no plaster added. Dry casein glue is best, but instead of this you can use dextrine or wheat paste, which is used in hanging wall paper. Dextrine makes the paste a little tougher than the wheat paste alone.

If you want to make a dry mix, add about 2 tablespoonfuls of dextrine or dry wheat paste to 1 pint of dry paper pulp and mix thoroughly. When you need a slow-setting mâché, this mixture can be used by just adding enough water to make it a doughlike consistency. If you want it to set faster, add as much plaster as necessary when you mix it up.

Formula #13: fish mix   Use for mounting fish as described in methods #1 and #2, Chapter 12.

Mix ground asbestos with dextrine solution, Formula #5, until the mixture is quite firm. Add dry molding plaster to this, a little at a time, and stir it in until it is about the consistency of thick dough.

Index

Boldface numbers refer to definitions; italic numbers refer to illustrations.